This wasn't her.
Every part of me knew tha
in her nature to do
This wasn't her.

THE
UNTHINKABLE

THE UNTHINKABLE

A STORY OF CONTROL, VIOLENCE AND MY MOTHER

DAVID CHALLEN

brazen

June 2025

First edition

David Challen is a domestic abuse campaigner. He successfully campaigned to free his mother in a landmark appeal that recognised the lifetime of coercive control she suffered. David continues to speak out against violence against women and girls and is an advisor to the Domestic Abuse Commissioner for England and Wales and an Ambassador for the Prison Advice and Care Trust (Pact) and the Employers' Initiative on Domestic Abuse (EIDA).

The Unthinkable is his first book.

This story is dedicated to the child I forgot
and for the mother I saw.

For John

First published in Great Britain in 2025 by Brazen, an imprint of
Octopus Publishing Group Ltd
Carmelite House
50 Victoria Embankment
London EC4Y 0DZ
www.octopusbooks.co.uk

An Hachette UK Company
www.hachette.co.uk

The authorized representative in the EEA is Hachette Ireland, 8 Castlecourt
Centre, Dublin 15, D15 XTP3, Ireland (email: info@hbgi.ie)

Hardback ISBN: 978-1-91424-026-3
Trade paperback ISBN: 978-1-91424-027-0
eISBN: 978-1-91424-029-4

A CIP catalogue record for this book is available from the British Library.

Typeset in 10.5/16pt Swift LT Std by Six Red Marbles UK, Thetford, Norfolk

Printed and bound in Great Britain.

3 5 7 9 10 8 6 4 2

This FSC® label means that materials used for the product
have been responsibly sourced.

The Unthinkable

Memories.

Some are familiar, their surfaces smoothed by the years until they fit into the palm of your hand, into your life story. Some are colossal and jagged, and you only rediscover them when you least expect to. And the really painful ones, well, you don't want to touch or see them ever again.

But how can you leave your past in the past if you haven't ever explored it? How can you survive memories you haven't held up to the light?

People often want to know what it was like, my childhood. Sometimes they ask me straight. Their voyeurism desires something they can hold up in front of them, hard and definite and grotesque. Something concrete. Something that explains it all. Something that confirms it won't happen to them.

But terrible things happen all the time. To everybody. To anybody. The unthinkable parts of life are sitting just below its surface. Waiting to trip you up.

Prologue

It began as a normal Sunday morning.

'Are you ready?' she said as she climbed into the driving seat of her red Ford Ka.

'Yeah, coming, Mum,' I called, shutting the front door and jumping into the passenger seat.

It was subdued in the car – the atmosphere of the overcast day weighed down on us. In good times my mum would have been chatty on these drives to my work, cajoling me into laughter. I would be more taciturn, trying to ready myself for yet another working day. I was twenty-three years old, and in an emotionally selfish phase. The pressure of a working day spent constantly forcing a smile onto my face for customers left me unavailable to her. But on this drive she didn't try to coax conversation out of me; instead she was lost in her own thoughts.

I was still living with her, but we weren't living in our real home. It was a new house, fifteen minutes' walk away from the old one where I had grown up with my parents and elder brother, James. Mum and I had moved there after my parents' marriage had gone through its death throes eighteen months ago. It was a quiet and soulless red brick house, hived off in a gated community. Inside it was sterile, more of a shelter than a place we could call home. Life ever since had felt an octave off-key; the house's furniture was different, flimsier, not the comfortable trappings of my childhood. Bog-standard flatpack furnishings to get us by until we started again. The leafy suburban streets and lanes were as known to us as each other, but we came at them now from the wrong direction. It was as though we had been trying on a different life for size, and it was the wrong fit.

Mum pulled up into one of the parking spaces outside the restaurant and I climbed out of the car, unthinkingly. Just as I turned to shut the door, she leaned over, right across the passenger seat, and looked me deep in the eyes. Her own blue eyes crinkled with intensity at mine, her mouth drawn downwards so that her lips almost disappeared. It was as though she was trying to locate and fix on something within me, trying to speak to the child still within.

'You know I love you, don't you, David?'

The cool of the car door handle was frigid in my clamped hand. This intensity was all off. I was used to hearing 'I love you', but this wasn't that. This was an opening, or a closing. But it was also 9.30am. My shift was starting, and I didn't want to be late.

'Yeah . . . yeah, of course. I love you too,' I said, turning to go.

But the unease didn't lift and it forced me to turn back to look at her, just once. She didn't return my gaze, and a frown was now etched across her face as she settled back into her seat, her lips still folded in on themselves. She had closed off.

By the time I reached the back entrance of the restaurant, she was gone. I didn't have time to cross-examine it, so I stitched a smile across my face, opened the doors and began my day.

*

A large party of eleven came in just as the lunchtime rush had slowed to a trickle of tables. I had already dealt with their complicated drinks order, and was readying myself to ask about food, when my manager appeared in front of me.

'David,' he said, 'do you mind heading up to the locker room for a moment? I need to speak to you. I'll be up in a minute; just wait for me there.'

'Yeah, sure,' I said, taken aback at his serious tone. I headed up the stairs into the locker room. Its heavy door with a porthole window shut heavily behind me. *I've been fine today, haven't I?* I thought. *No tables complaining, nothing massively delayed . . .* And it was there, pacing around the hot little upstairs room, that I caught a glimpse of something shocking through the window: heading towards me at speed was my mum's cousin, Noel. And looming behind her was the hi-vis jacket of a police officer.

My sense of space and time loosened with the shock and knowledge that something very bad was about to happen. I was a child again, hurtling through space, knowing I had fallen, waiting for the pain to hit.

And then time sped; Noel had me by the shoulders. She was forcing words out, forcing them into my comprehension:

'David.

Your

dad's

been

found

dead.'

The air around me screamed.

I threw anything within reach on the floor.

Your dad's been found dead.

Now I was on the ground. Flailing.

The last words I had said to him; the insults.

Noel caught me round the waist. My body resisted my mind. My hands burning from the blow after blow I was raining onto the thin metal of the surrounding lockers. A policeman at the door, waiting.

. . . I am gathering my stuff from my locker . . .

. . . now I'm downstairs, still wearing my apron, I can't find my uniform hat . . .

. . . now I'm in front of my familiar station, fumbling to hand over my work stuff, in tears . . .

. . . I can't start a sentence, finish a sentence, utter a single word . . .

. . . My hands are shaking and someone, somewhere, is saying *it's fine . . . don't worry . . . don't worry . . .*

. . . I'm standing in the middle of the packed restaurant with a police officer at my shoulder . . .

. . . outside it's afternoon and rain is falling, there is a police car parked in the side road, and I am getting into the back . . .

. . .none of it computes.

My father's body.

Found.

Where is my mother?

Somewhere through the seething mass of static, the words:

'Beachy Head'.

My mother is there,

she is on a clifftop,
ready to jump,
and people are trying to talk her down.
. . . *my father is dead.*
Were they jumping together?
She is still alive . . .
he jumped and she didn't?
But.
He was found at our home . . .

The police car drives us to Noel's house. I curl up on the sofa in the bay window of her sitting room, marooned. A police officer stands at the door, walkie-talkie crackling intermittently, his uniformed presence a looming spectre.

I will never get out of this room.

The entire gravity of my world shifts to Mum.

Can they rescue her?

Will she jump?

Everything I have stands on that precipice with her.

But she is still here, and I am still here.

We are both still in this world at this moment.

She wouldn't let me and my brother go.

She loves us too much.

She won't leave us.

Will she?

Time collapses into one singular point all around me.

Here are the things I didn't know then.

On Saturday 14 August 2010, the day before, my mother had gone to see my father at our old family home in the morning. They were clearing out the garage together. She had been attempting a reconciliation in spite of their separation and his treatment of her. That reconciliation came with strange conditions he had set. And still she went over. Her need for him overwhelmed everything else.

Dad insisted she go out to buy some ingredients to make him lunch. Used to taking his orders, she trekked out to the local shops in the pouring rain.

As she was cooking and serving up bacon and eggs at home, she noticed that the home phone had been moved. She dialled 1471, to check the number of the last caller, and listened to the automated voice spiel out the number of a woman that she knew he had been seeing since their separation.

As Dad ate the lunch she had made him, she asked him, 'Am I going to see you tomorrow?'

'No.'

'Why?'

'Don't question me, Sally,' he had replied.

And with those words, my quiet and fearful mother picked up a hammer and hit him. More than twenty times to the head. She then went upstairs to change out of her bloodied clothes.

When she came back down to the kitchen, she covered his now-lifeless body with some old curtains, wrote a note and placed it on top of him.

I love you. Sally.

Before leaving, she cleared and washed up his dirty pans and dishes. When she arrived back at the new house we were living in together, she typed up a longer note and printed it out, changed her clothes again, and returned to our old home's kitchen once more to leave the new note on his covered body.

When I got into her car the next morning, Mum had already placed a little plastic stepping stool behind my passenger seat. After dropping me off at work, she had driven for two hours to Beachy Head. When she reached the car park, she called Noel and told her what she had done to my father, and gave her numbers for my brother and me, asking her to pick me up from work.

She hung up and got out of the car, taking the little stool with her, which she used to climb over the fences between her and the cliff edge. She then headed out along the headland to find a spot to jump from.

A chaplain who often patrolled the cliffs for jumpers spotted her. She tried to get away from him, but he followed her to a precipice and tried to talk her down.

Noel didn't do as she was told.

She called the police, who went round to our family home, broke down the front door, and found my father on the kitchen floor, just as my mother had described.

I have no clear memory of when I realised my mother was responsible for the death of my father. I can't remember those sentences coming out of anybody's mouth. It was a knowledge without words, a creeping build-up of unthinkable certainty.

My mother was the cornerstone of my morality. She was kind and compassionate; my guiding shepherd.

This wasn't her.

Every part of me knew that. It wasn't in her nature to do

this. Let alone to my father, who she'd always loved in spite of everything.

This wasn't her.

That night, I dreamed in vivid technicolour that my father was standing at the foot of my bed. I was trying to tell him about my life, my hopes and ambitions, pouring it all out.

Whatever I said, however I tried to reach him, he just stood there, in silence. Unmoving. Unreachable. It was a feeling that was horribly familiar.

And then I woke up, and I was alone in the room, and he was gone.

BEFORE

Chapter One

Sometimes, when I think about my home, my childhood, I grasp for the golden moments.

I am six or seven, kneeling on the carpeted floor of our living room and playing a game with my mother. She's sitting facing away from the main doors to the living room, and from behind me I hear my dad come in. I look up at her as she turns towards him and see happiness swimming across her face as she recognises what is in his hands: a small black box. Opening it, she beams with joy and pulls out a heavy gold necklace. My father smiles at her reaction as he reaches behind her neck to help her put it on, threading his arms under her shining blond hair. Their togetherness, the intensity of it, I feel inside myself.

But however much I search my memory, that togetherness is a one-off. They would never be like that again.

When I was little, I used to love looking through our photo albums, seeing the story of our family.

There were my parents at their wedding, an English garden on a sunlit day. My mother, only 24, with loose hair, smiling in a high-necked dress. My father, dark-haired and grinning, twining his hands into hers.

Then, as the years pass, there is a family, the four of us grinning up from the photos outside a perfect-looking family house. It was a secluded four-bedroom house perched at the top of a road, Ruxley Ridge, in the small, leafy Surrey village of Claygate. The long driveway burrowed down into the land the house sat on, and from the road you could almost see right into all four corners of our house. But my favourite place was the back garden, where I had a little white Wendy house with a red trim on the roof. There I am in the pictures: it's a sunny, bright day and I am in a red plastic car, pedalling as fast as I can, laughing. My mother isn't in the picture but I know she is near. She loved the garden, loved weeding and digging up bulbs, stopping occasionally to call to our cat Tiggy, who she adored. He would be hiding in the bushes waiting for her call before darting out to greet her.

Beyond the garden and the Wendy house lay deep bushes and rhododendrons with an opening hidden within the leaves, a little hideaway from where I would secretly watch my family. Further still lay a deep, wild area with tall, spindly trees. It was a square of land belonging to no one, left untouched and uncharted, and at night it was dark and terrifying. On rare occasions, deep into the evening, I would spot the small shape of an owl there, a harbinger of the darker world outside the glowing warmth of our home. I felt safe on my side of the glass.

Mum stayed at home for the first half of my childhood. She and I would often explore together in a small wood at the bottom of our road. She would watch as I cycled down the dips and up the humps of the dirt-bike track. In autumn, the woods were an ideal foraging ground for conkers, and my exploits would always leave me with splinters in my fingers. Late afternoons were then spent at my mother's dressing table as she kneeled in front of me, pulling them out one by one with tweezers.

As a child, I was bursting with life, always moving, always talking. There was a brightness in me, a kind of boundless energy that I couldn't contain. I had a head full of dreams, one minute wanting to be a soldier, the next a vet, then an architect.

I would dress up in little military outfits, saluting around the house, or sit glued to the television, enchanted by films, eager to recount every scene to my mum. She loved it, indulging my stories, questions and endless chatter. There was a warmth to those days. Even simple car rides felt special with her. Windows down, our voices would tangle together as the music rotated through the CD player. Prince's 'Little Red Corvette' tied with REM's 'Losing My Religion', her all-time favourite. Freddy Mercury would declare 'It's a Kind of Magic,' or Tina Turner would belt out 'Nutbush City Limits' with Mum in full-voiced support.

'Look at you, David, singing every note!' she would say, turning to me with a huge smile. It was just us, and I felt safe.

She would take me on errands to The Parade in Claygate. She stopped to talk to everyone we encountered, from the family who ran the newsagents to the bakers, where, if I was lucky, she'd buy me a chocolate-dipped Viennese whirl. On supermarket trips I would race to find my favourite cookie from the bakery counter, always a giant double-chocolate cookie wrapped in cellophane. I would make a game of trying to sneak a bite before we reached the checkout, only to be betrayed by its crinkly rustling noise.

She taught me to swim at the Kingfisher Centre in Leatherhead, the vast, echoey indoor pool leaving me with the taste of chlorine on my skin. Sometimes she'd suggest an even larger adventure, like the beach at Camber Sands a few hours' drive away. And once a year we went to the annual Flower Show on the common, where the large, desolate green would be transformed by cream-coloured tarpaulin tents and music from marching bands.

These small moments in time were sewn into the fabric of my childhood. They felt impossible to spoil.

My early memories of Dad come separately. He was a successful businessman, an entrepreneur who had built his second-hand car business from the ground up. He had started out as a sole trader, selling cars out of a rented flat, and by the time I was a child, he had his own showroom. He was good at his job, people liked him, and until I was about five, he was a doting father who would playfully pinch my cheeks and coo 'Little David' as I cuddled tightly up to him on the sofa.

He helped me tie my shoelaces, showing me the dance – up and over, under and through. But if I failed, he would leave, looking to Mum to help me rather than kneel down himself.

And as I grew older, something shifted. It was a slow, almost imperceptible change, like a tide pulling away without anyone noticing. Dad, who once burst through the door, eyes searching for me to grab and pull me up, suddenly stopped looking. One day I was the bright thing he reached for, and the next, I was part of the background. There was a wrongness I couldn't explain. I don't remember when and how it happened, but I remember the thud within me. It wasn't just the loss; it was how readily I accepted it. Something in my stomach felt different. Because he felt different.

It felt like I had outgrown my purpose in his life, and the fact I was discarded sat quietly inside me.

That's when I started to notice the fog. I couldn't hold it in my hand. I couldn't clearly describe it. It didn't fit into the shape of words, but the atmosphere changed. Something noxious crept in and filled the rooms of our home.

Over time, the house on Ruxley Ridge became like a doll's house in which the little figures kept to their own particular spaces. There was us, and there was my Dad, and the spaces in between us felt too vast, too unreachable.

The living room was Dad's territory, where you'd find him in the evenings or on Sundays, with Formula One or MotoGP on the television. The racers ticked left and right, in and out of the corners of the huge plasma screen, tyres glued to the tarmac. Dad's rimless glasses would wink in the light of the TV as he followed them.

Often, he would ignore any attempt to engage with him while he was watching TV. Or, if you came into the living room part way through a programme, he would pick up the remote to mute before slamming it down and ask, 'Are you in, or are you out? Decide!'

He had bought the TV off a friend and spent a fortune mounting it on a wall. He didn't like people watching it without him, complaining it 'curtailed its lifespan'. Using the DVD player was an even greater offence. This was all his property and not for our use.

So it was clear that the living room was Dad's territory.

Meanwhile, my mother's domain was the kitchen, on the other side of the house. She was a great cook – there was always something delicious to eat at the kitchen table.

Every Sunday afternoon Mum could be found marshalling a hot stove with rows of old stainless-steel pans, the edges burnt, dented and worn. They seemed vast from my small height and sat simmering, brimming with goodness as I lingered in the doorway, watching. One afternoon, Mum looked over at me.

'David, do you want to learn how to cook a roast?' she asked.

The idea of learning something so grownup felt enormous. Within moments I was sitting up on a chair, painstakingly peeling a bagful of potatoes, trying not to catch my fingers and thumbs as my hands fumbled with excitement.

Then Dad walked in. Somehow, his presence pierced a cold stake through the warmth of the moment.

'Oh, you're learning to cook,' he grinned, leaning down to my ear. 'Good. You can help your mother in the kitchen. It'll be useful to have another pair of little hands. She's always saying she hasn't got enough time.'

He was smiling, but his words had an up-to-no-good air about them, an off-kilter edge. I could feel them needling into me, the tone sharper than their meaning.

Mum didn't say anything. Her eyes were set on stewarding the pans that grumbled away in front of her. Then he left, and the air uncoiled slightly. But the warmth between us had shifted into a flatness. She looked back at me, her smile gentle but distinctly thinner now. Muted.

*

Mum's day-to-day life became a timed assault course of challenges when I was twelve and she started working full time as an office manager at the Police Federation of England, supporting 43 forces. After picking me up from school and cleaning and cooking for her mum, Granny Jenney, the second shift – running the home – would begin. Weaving her way through the house, she was always on the way to one chore or another, before preparing dinner for all the family.

Occasionally we would all eat together, but Dad would often get irritated. If my brother or I held my knife and fork the 'wrong' way, his head would angrily pan round to my mother: 'Why don't you teach these children table manners?' There was never any question that he would teach us. While she was a cook, a cleaner and an after-school tutor, Dad's responsibilities, to both the household and the family unit, ended at the front door.

So, adding to Mum's burden, most nights became two-dinner nights. She would make dinner for the three of us and cook again for Dad when he came home around 8 or 9pm. If she was running behind schedule, he would stand imposingly in the entrance to the kitchen: 'Sally, why isn't dinner ready? You knew what time I was coming home. I don't understand why it's not on the table.'

Mum would hover over the stove, anxiously manoeuvring her way round pots and pans. 'I'm sorry, I've had a lot to do today, it'll be ready in 10 minutes, I promise.'

The idea that he could make food for himself never arose. Dad was in charge; he brought in the money. Everything else, Mum took care of. Mum was the engine of the house, Dad was the captain. And his word was law. He never had a list or an explicit set of rules or punishments. He didn't have to: we all instinctively knew where the lines were. And we followed them.

But Mum's duties didn't stop with the housework. Because Dad didn't trust anyone, he never employed help in the garage. It was Mum's duty to do the business accounts, and she would work for hours on weekends in the office upstairs, a large brown leather book in front of her. He'd insist on paying the business's taxes in cash, so that once a year, her domain of the kitchen table was taken over with towering piles of notes. That was the way he ordained it.

It was also Mum's job to drive him to collect the cars he had bought. 'Sally, I need you to help me pick up a car in Guildford,' he would spontaneously announce a couple of times a week. 'Don't argue about it now, come on.'

It was an instruction. Mum's body would sink a little; I would look up at her pleadingly.

'Do your homework, David. I can look at it when I come back,' she would say consolingly.

'But when are you coming back?' I'd reply.

'I'm sorry.' And with that, she would walk out. There was never any warning or discussion, and it would take hours sometimes.

With her gone, loneliness would fill the corners of the room. When she left, the house fell into shadow. The street was always so silent – no children, no laughter. Doors closed tight.

Chapter Two

My parents met young, introduced by way of their mutual friend Del, who my mother had been on two dates with as a teenager. Del had dumped her for another girlfriend, but not before my father had seen her one day at Del's parents' house.

Until then, Mum had led a sheltered life in a large and rather colourful family. My Granny Jenney had been raised in India. The daughter of a powerful Commissioner, Granny had witnessed the dying embers of British colonial rule and the horrific bloodshed of Partition. She spun tales for me about the pet monkey she used to adore and the local maharaja who tried to gift her a baby elephant – a gift that was blocked by her father, who could not be accused of showing favouritism. She could speak Urdu, and recite word-for-word reams of long poems.

Mum's father had been part of the Royal Engineers in India, and together they'd had four children: Brian, Terence, Nigel and – a full ten years later – my mum. When Mum's father died before she turned five, Granny Jenney was left a widow. Worried that Sally would be lonely, since she was so much younger than her brothers, Granny took the unusual decision to adopt a son near Mum's age, Christopher, to keep her company.

Granny Jenney's charming little house always felt like home to me, more so than Ruxley Ridge, which felt increasingly empty as I got older, despite its show-home exterior. Granny's house was like something from a story book, with rose bushes in the garden, a sweet little wooden door and a cosy fireplace surrounded by flower-embroidered chairs. Most days my mother would drive us there to spend the afternoon. Granny would fuss over me, making me boiled eggs with toasted soldiers.

Mum had first invited Dad back home after he – remembering their meeting at Del's house – had gone into the newspaper shop where she worked to chat her up. Granny Jenney had recognised him as the salesman who had once sold her a car, and commented that he was very full of himself. I was later told that Granny Jenney had been keener on a young man from Mum's ballroom dancing classes, but Mum didn't find him attractive. And Granny even told Mum that she trusted Del, and thought he would be a man who would treat her well. Not like my father.

Mum's was an upper-middle-class family – the brothers went to Oxford or Cambridge universities, and got the respectable jobs that come with that, all suited and self-assured. Somehow I always sensed my mother's family looking a little askance at my father's job and his background. His business was thriving and he was doing well, but he was just not their sort of person. Still, Mum persevered with the relationship, but when he proposed about a year in, and with Mum still at school, she answered: 'We'll have to wait.'

After that, the family even tried to separate my parents, sending Mum to my uncle Terence's in Brussels to attend a finishing school there. None of it worked. Mum returned just as desperately in love with Dad as she ever had been. But after that first proposal, Dad waited a long time before proposing again. Mum told me she had been longing for him to ask. They finally married ten years after they met, and four years after that – a long wait, according to my mother – my brother arrived. Mum had defied her family's wishes, but she always remained close with her mother and brothers.

Throughout my childhood, an annual highlight was Noel's Christmas party at her lovely big family home in Hampton Court. It felt like a private gentlemen's club, smoky, loud and free-flowing with drink. The whole of Mum's family would gather, fuelled by port, wine and cheese, the scent of the café noir cigarillos that her brothers smoked hovering in the air. The mahogany-panelled walls would glow in the soft light, and it was always too full to move easily across the room. Mum would shine with happiness at being with her family, and I loved hanging around near her and watching her light up.

It was rare for my father to go to these parties, or to visit Granny Jenney's house. Even as a child, I somehow knew that there had been an incident early on where Mum's brothers had confronted Dad at his house. My mother's large, sprawling family, confident in its position in the world, was a contrast to his own, I knew. There was a reason why he kept away.

I just didn't know what it was yet.

Chapter Three

In March 1998, we went to Los Angeles to stay with my parents' friend Del.

On arrival, he greeted us at the door. To ten-year-old me, Del's sprawling house, with views down the hills into Los Angeles' centre, was like something out of the movies – all on one level, with a pool table inside. Most tempting of all was his swimming pool. I loved swimming. I would hover in the silence beneath the surface, the world and its noise retreating further and further away.

The adults all got on well and Dad and Del could talk cars for hours.

But there was also something off about that holiday. It didn't quite live up to the sunshine-drenched Californian dream, with showery weather and a sad trip to the SeaWorld theme park, where we didn't see anything. And there was an underlying sense of discomfort that I couldn't put my finger on.

I think it began with a trip to Universal Studios, courtesy of an ex-girlfriend of Dad's. It seemed Mum hadn't been made aware of this connection in advance, and as the ex-girlfriend led Dad through a special entrance to the park, with Mum, James and me in tow, the silence between us all was tangible.

Then 1 April arrived: my birthday. Finally, the holiday started to feel like a celebration. We had visited a camera shop a few days before, an Aladdin's cave of treasure to me, and I had fallen in love with a white telescope on its crowded shelves. I had always been fascinated by the huge unknown of space and its vast expanses.

On the morning of my birthday that gleaming white telescope was waiting for me as a present. I could barely wait for evening, when we started setting it up on Del's patio by the pool, calibrating and recalibrating it until we managed to find the moon hanging low over the LA skyline. I went to bed that night happy, the glowing lump of rock huge in my mind's eye.

But the next day, I knew something was wrong as soon as I opened my eyes. Yesterday, I had woken to the reassuring noises of breakfast being cooked and plans being made. Today, I was met with a deadening silence.

I walked outside to see all the adults arguing by the pool. Dad and Del were both shouting, but I couldn't make out their words.

I ran back to my guest room to hide, not knowing what was going on, but feeling like I shouldn't be witnessing it. When I eventually came out again, Mum had disappeared. James joined me in my room and I asked him over and over: 'What's happening? Why can't I see Mum? What's going on?' But all he could say was that we had to stay where we were.

Later that morning, Dad called James out of the room and spoke to him privately. He came back looking blank.

'What happened?' I asked.

More silence. A dark, strange mood threaded through every room in the house.

And then we were told that the holiday was over. It felt

like a safety drill. Exit please. Get your stuff. Leave. Eyes forward. Don't interact. There was no discussion, no appeal. My father had decreed it, and it was happening. His anger moved us all around like chess pieces on his board.

My mother was oddly diminished as we left. Del was standing at the front of the house as we put our bags into the trunk. Dad swept past without acknowledging his presence. Rain fell as we left. The LA skies were heavy above us – you couldn't see past the clouds any more.

I watched Del through the rearview mirror, getting smaller and smaller until it was just the four of us in the car. There was no shouting, but we were all suffocated by Dad's anger.

James finally told me what had happened. Apparently, Mum and Del had been having a drink together in the living room. Dad had walked in as Del went to kiss her, and Dad had gone ballistic.

I couldn't get my head around it. Why would Del kiss my mum?

Back at home, nobody spoke about the trip – we all pretended it had never happened. The only trace of it was in Mum's behaviour. She was quieter, more subdued. And, I noticed, she was no longer wearing the gold necklace that Dad had given her.

Something dark had been born on that holiday. The strange feeling I had about Dad became a weight inside me.

I never looked up at the sky with the telescope again.

'After Los Angeles, the heavy atmosphere stayed with us. And then, months later, something happened that was connected with the incident at Del's in ways I wouldn't understand until years later. A family trip to *Star Wars: The Phantom Menace* was planned, which I was really looking forward to. Leicester Square was teeming with excitement. There were hundreds of people dressed up as Darth Vader and Jedi warriors, light sabre battles going on all around us, celebration in the air. But I was staring at the ground, confused. I knew I shouldn't ask, but I couldn't keep it in.

'Dad, why isn't Mum here?'

His head was swivelling left and right, busily searching for a way through the masses.

'She's busy, she couldn't come,' he replied curtly, not even glancing in my direction.

It didn't make sense. Mum was never busy without Dad. But his manner made it totally clear: leave it alone.

For some reason, Mum had not been allowed to come. It would be a long time before I discovered why.

Chapter Four

The atmosphere at our house on Ruxley Ridge had become watched and loaded.

At friends' houses, I looked on in surprise as their parents gave each other a natural-looking kiss or hug for no reason. It felt odd to me, and far too much. That kind of thing did not happen in our house. Yes, sure, my mum would sometimes go for a kiss or a hug, but Dad would slide out from under it, as though what she was offering was a childish whim. Love flowed one way in our house: from Mum.

Dad's game had always been mercy-mercy. He would stand in the middle of a room, his stance gladiatorial, a playful grin on his face. Splaying out both hands in front of him, he would goad us into battle. The game would be to interlock hands, the aim being to bend your opponent's hand back and twist it until they couldn't bear it any longer. I always hoped it would be fun. It never was. There was no letting up because he was bigger than us. And he wanted to win. It left me confused. In other homes when dads reached out it was a show of love; in mine it became a merciless game.

More usual were Dad's flashes of anger. His mood would deteriorate over the smallest thing. If my mother cooked food he didn't like, he'd ask, looking down at his plate disgustedly, 'Why have you given me this?' Mum's face would fall, her eyes and mouth slanting downwards.

If it wasn't outright anger, Dad would belittle Mum and her contributions in other ways. In contrast to Dad's hoarding of resources, for her, watching TV was about sharing: 'Oh, that's that lady who was in the drama we watched last week, do you remember?' Dad would mute the TV ostentatiously, shaming her into silence. 'Sally. Are you going to talk all the way through this? Because I'd like to watch it.'

On occasion I would join in with her, chatting excitedly back-and-forth, only to receive the same darts of ire from Dad.

Mum loved to tell stories around the dinner table, but if she talked 'too much', she would be trampled over by my father.

'That's enough, Sally,' he would say with finality.

Mum would simply stare in front of her, pretending he hadn't spoken. Or if she was feeling brave, she might turn to me, looking exasperated. I would wince. I couldn't bear him talking to her like that.

There was a knife-like quality to his silencing, her mortification radiating out so everybody in the room felt the sharpness and cruelty of his tongue.

My parents would sometimes have dinner parties or barbecues with our neighbours, the Cowdys. We children would watch TV in Jack Cowdy's den while our parents drank wine and gathered in the garden. Sometimes, when it was just an adult dinner party, my mum still would take me along, and I would sit in a corner listening to the ebb and flow of grown-up conversation. I enjoyed these fly-on-the-wall moments, studiously watching the adults interact, and I noticed how my mum came alive in a social setting. It was on occasions like this that I saw her at her brightest, and I loved it.

But I would also see how, when she got into full flow, Dad's eyes would flit quickly backwards and forwards in her direction. He was trying to get her attention, to shut her up.

He had a way of handing out small moments of humiliation under the guise of humour. 'Thunder thighs,' he would call her at the table. 'You don't want to see her naked!' he'd proclaim with a wide grin across his face. 'You can't even fit into your clothes.'

Nobody else found it funny – I could see that. He was goading them as well as her, not caring that it made people uncomfortable. He took great pleasure in this lawlessness and reckless moral abandon. As for me, I felt immobilised. There was never a thought of speaking out. I lived – we all lived – inside his boundaries.

When his parents died, Dad used the inheritance to treat himself to something he had dreamt of since childhood: a Ferrari. He had always loved motorsports, and had even wanted to become a racing car driver when he was growing up. But his own father, Keith, had been the first motoring correspondent for the News of the World, known and respected by all the motoring legends – and he wouldn't hear of it. He knew only too well how dangerous a career it was. Perhaps the Ferrari was a nod to his memory.

It sat on the driveway, brash and red, garlanded with all sorts of expensive extras – F1 gear changing, black grille on the rear bonnet, red callipers – and a raft of lifestyle benefits. He joined the Ferrari Owners' Club and started to travel round Europe with his new friends, taking Mum along for the ride. Wearing a Ferrari hat and the race team shirt, Dad would load their suitcases into the tiny front trunk, and off they would drive. He was embracing a new life now, and at first I thought it was a midlife crisis: buying a garish sports car, dying his hair and dressing in linen suits and trendy outfits. There was new lease of life about him, a spring in his step.

Owning the Ferrari only seemed to deepen the pleasure he took in breaking the rules. One evening, when he'd had it about a year, Dad got caught speeding on a bridge not far from home, with me in the car. As the officer walked up to the driver's door, I saw a familiar look descend over Dad's face. He was excited for the head-to-head that was about to happen. He faced obstinately forward in silence, avoiding all interaction as the officer spoke and handed him the paperwork.

'All the information to pay is on the slip. Have a good evening,' the officer said as he left.

'We'll see about that,' Dad said under his breath as he rolled up his windows. He looked unperturbed, almost ecstatic. Speeding tickets would always find a way to disappear, like any other bill he didn't want to pay.

The Ferrari represented a sort of identity overhaul for my father. He did everything he could to live up to it. I'd catch glimpses of him covering it up in its silky red car cover, tucking it in at night. At times, that car felt like a member of the family, something new to dote on and care for.

One December, when I was 16, I heard an argument emanating from the kitchen. I went in to find Mum in tears, head bowed over something in her hand: a Christmas card, professionally printed in full colour.

'Merry Christmas!' it read in snow-topped red and green letters. Beneath was a photo of Dad dressed in trousers and a dark, low-cut shirt, sitting on the bonnet of the Ferrari, its famous rearing horse logo visible between his spread-eagled legs. Flanking him on either side were two blonde models, entirely naked apart from black stilettos, with their arms draped across his shoulders. Each had a hand resting on his thigh, and he had his arms round their waists. It read: 'From Richard and the 'Service' Department at Westlake Garage.' Without telling Mum, he had sent these cards to everyone they knew. She was distraught.

To me, it felt like Dad's behaviour had shifted gears, as though the boundaries of normal behaviour were falling away.

He was openly taking her down in front of us, diminishing her spirit, bit by bit. And the humiliation was beginning to affect us all.

At times, the atmosphere at home felt like an invisible fire whose heat you could always feel. In that moment it had flickered in my face.

The following year he did it again.

A month or two into the new year, I overheard the two of them arguing, this time in the living room. I went in to see Dad place a framed photograph on the centre of the bookcase: the Christmas card.

He was smiling as he did it, testing how far he could push her.

'You can't put that there,' said Mum. 'I won't let you.'

'Why not?' he asked. 'Why can't I?'

I was getting older now, almost an adult. I couldn't loiter on the sidelines anymore, so I stepped in. 'Is this a joke? Of course you can't put that there, Dad. It's you with two naked women. You can't put it anywhere, let alone in our home.'

He smiled back at me, his mouth open in mock surprise.

I stood beside Mum, refusing to break eye contact.

Next to me I could feel her panic. 'Why are you doing this, Richard? Why?' she repeated.

My mind was racing with the same questions.

Why?

Why was he taking such pleasure at her distress?

Why was he smiling back at me?

Eventually, he relented, but his grin grew wider than ever. He had won again because both of us were shaken. It felt like the temperature in the home had been racked up. There was something obscene about this new game he had concocted, as though he was trying to pervert our fundamental understanding of right and wrong.

Fast cars, fast living had become Dad's goal. Mum had always been discouraged from socialising alone; she could only do it when he was by her side. But by my late teens, my parents never saw their old friends anymore. Fractures had formed in those relationships, though I never knew why. Rather than attending local dinner parties, where Mum would light up in the social environment, she became simply an accessory on Dad's Ferrari holidays, tucked inside his flashy car. Dad's new persona seemed to cage her, like a bird whose wings were clipped.

Dad hated being told what to do.

One year, he drove his Ferrari on a track day at Spa in Belgium. Refusing the official's guidance and their offer to show him the ropes, Dad insisted on finding his way round the track himself. He lost control and nearly totalled the car into a wall. Miraculously, he walked away unhurt, but he was furious at having to pay for the damage caused to the track. The Ferrari was written off, never to return.

On returning to the UK, it transpired that the damages were not insured, as he hadn't told the insurers that he was taking the car abroad. Unwilling, once again, to deal with the consequences, he concocted a plan to return the car to the UK, where he would report to the police that a lorry had smashed into it.

His plan failed. The insurance company investigation discovered his story was fraudulent, and Dad was arrested and charged. His defence in court was that he hadn't appreciated the seriousness of his actions, and he said that the shame had consumed him so much that he had lost two stone in weight. As far as I could see, he didn't care in the slightest.

I should have been scared, perhaps relieved. The law had finally caught up with him. But I was neither; I knew the rules didn't apply. Getting caught didn't change that for him, or for us.

But he got what he wanted: a slap on the wrist, no jail time, a suspended sentence and 100 hours of community service working in a charity shop. He came back from it one night cock-a-hoop: someone had handed in a good Armani suit – which he had snaffled for himself.

Chapter Five

Just as Dad managed to pile humiliation upon humiliation on Mum's shoulders, so he gradually battered down any confidence I had. The happy, chatty boy, brimming over with imagination, was slowly morphing into someone quieter, more diminished. Someone who would take up less space.

The more I tried to reach for Dad, the more I lost any sense of who I was.

Back when I was small, he would take us to the local track with an old go-kart, and later to circuits like Brands Hatch for Ferrari Owners' Club events. On family days like these we felt seen, involved – so at Brands Hatch, I wanted to show willing by having a go at driving when he asked.

The last time I tried it, I'd barely got out of the car before I was sick. Unable to get the cumbersome helmet off in time, I vomited into it, the bile mixed with panic. Then came the fear. I could barely look up. The disdain radiated off Dad like heat.

I didn't speak. Instead, I hobbled off to the bathroom, knowing I had disappointed him.

At Brands Hatch, traders would be scattered about the garages, selling their wares. As he walked me down to the race-track pits, I could see a lone glass display box with a watch inside that was technical and expensive-looking. Dad pointed at it. 'That watch is the cost of our holiday,' he said.

Silence again. I wasn't sure how to react.

I felt, as I'm sure he intended, that I was a burden on him, weighing him down – and always would be.

Throughout my primary education, the surface of our home felt perfectly kept, untouched by the outside world. Shuttling to and from school we were the picture of an upper-middle-class family with two-point-four children and all the trappings of a well-ordered family life. But in reality, Dad rarely involved himself in anything to do with us.

At age eleven I played for the school's football B team. On match days, a cohort of dads would usually turn up, gesticulating enthusiastically from the sidelines. But for one match –a cold, wet, away game – no parents showed up to watch. Midway through the first half, however, as I moved up the pitch with the team and helped press our attack, I looked back to see Dad standing by our goal.

Peering through the slicing rain, I thought I must be wrong. But it was him: big coat, frameless glasses and goatee, stern-faced, hands in his pockets. He was groomed and serious, smartly dressed. He had never come to any games before. He had given no warning. *Why was he here?* I tried to feel excited by his presence, but it felt too foreign. He didn't acknowledge me in the slightest. There was no smile.

As he studied me, I revved up my game, taking on lots of tackles and winning them all. I ran forward with the ball and completed passes. But when I had a chance to look up again, he was gone. *Did I not play well enough?*

Neither Dad nor I spoke about it afterwards. I had let him down.

*

By my secondary school years, Dad seemed to have completely washed his hands of my upbringing.

One morning during the holidays, he was still in the house when I got up, sitting in his place at the head of the table. The kitchen was quiet, and sunlight shone across on the table as he sat flicking through a newspaper. He was about to turn the page when he looked up at me.

'Isn't this a day when you're supposed to be in school?' he said, his face ruffled by the knowledge that he wasn't alone. I looked at him without surprise. This had happened before.

'It's the summer holidays, Dad . . . I've not been at school for three weeks.'

A pause. He raised his eyebrows slightly, shrugged, and went back to his toast. I looked away, realising deep down what I already knew. He had no interest in my life, he had no idea what was going on in it – and what hurt the most was that I had long since accepted it.

During term time, I had never expected to see him at the school gates. When my mother had to go away for conferences with work, she was forced to order taxis to collect me from school because he'd refuse to pick me up. While the other children were met by their parents, I was picked up by a strange man in a suit. Shuffling into the back, I would try not to feel the eyes of the other kids on my back. Dad's just busy. He's hardly got any time for himself, I would reason.

But one day, sometime after he got the Ferrari, I was waiting for Mum after school when I heard it. That low, guttural growl of an engine. Heads turned before it even appeared. Teachers, children and their parents all stopped, their heads swivelling round. It was the Ferrari, loud and unapologetic. Alarms rang throughout my body, teenage embarrassment flooding me. I bolted to get in, keeping my head down, hoping I wouldn't be seen.

Dad didn't acknowledge me, nor even look at me. Instead, his eyes were busily fixed elsewhere. I watched him, and I could see his eyes scan the pavement, left to right, flicking through the faces . . . *He's looking for an audience*, I realised.

His face held a still, taut pride, as if he had something to prove. As the car slowly rolled forward, I buried myself deeper into the footwell, realising that none of this was for my benefit. School pick-up was just another theatre for him to show off his car.

That year, I started at a new school. It was four times as big as my last and friendship groups were already established, but its saving grace was its big, well-resourced music department. My dad, a big Keith Richards and Eric Clapton fan, paid for my extra guitar lessons there. I took them very seriously, and so did he.

He would walk into the playroom at home, coffee in hand, as I practised. I would duly try and pick something out. My head would ache over the guitar neck, my eyes focused hard on my fingers as they anchored themselves on the frets. I wanted to make him proud and show him what his money had bought.

But the longer he stood over me, the heavier my head felt. Errors sounded louder as I squirmed through difficult passages or tried to avoid them altogether.

'Why don't you ever play the solos like the record?' he

would say, almost snarling in dissatisfaction. Then he would walk out, leaving me in the wash of his disappointment. I knew he was judging me against some score card in his head, and I was failing.

He was showing a rare interest in me, and music felt like a way back to him. But it became a pre-ordained ceremony of shame. Eventually, I started messing up on purpose to make him walk out quicker. Any joy I took in music was washed away.

Still, I kept pursuing it. Somewhere inside me it felt like a kind of bridge by which I could reach him. And I learned to navigate his moods the way I learned to tune my guitar: by ear, adjusting instinctively, always listening for the slightest shift in dissonance.

Cooking had always felt like safety for me. It felt like togetherness: time with Mum, time with Granny Jenney. I knew every utensil, pot and pan my mum used, some of which were passed down from Granny after she died. Her favourite one was a special long, thin knife. Granny had used that knife for everything: testing consistency, needling into chickens and, most notably, for the indulgent butter fudge she made in an old pre-war baking tin. I learned alongside her, doing what she did. This was a world I knew and understood, and one I could get right.

When I was 14, my uncle John, Dad's older brother, came to visit from Australia. He was a quieter person than Dad, but still a character. Mum and I loved how he'd always arrive in the dead of winter dressed in shorts. He took a keen interest in what I was up to, and one evening I was telling him how much I loved to cook. I could feel Dad radiating again, taking issue at the head of the table. 'So, what can you cook, then?' he interrupted. I knew that tone, it meant he was spoiling for a fight. I could feel him circling, poised to pick me to shreds.

'Well, anything really. I like following recipes and making new things,' I replied.

'Yes, but that's following a recipe, isn't it? What can you actually cook?'

'Following a recipe *is* cooking, Dad. I don't know what you mean.'

He persisted with his head cocked menacingly. 'It's not though, is it? You're following a recipe. Following a recipe isn't cooking, I could do that.'

He stared me down. A silence settled on the table. As I looked around for help, I saw Uncle John bow his head with cowed resignation.

'You can't *actually* cook, can you, David?' The tone was now cutting, brutal.

I disappeared inside myself, knowing that this was the side of Dad you stayed clear of. His incredulous tone was perfectly pitched to humiliate you. John's head was still bowed.

A realisation came to me: Dad was a bully.

Bullying had become a huge problem for me.

At school, boys who had been good friends had started ostentatiously leaving me out of things. Left alone, I became a target for other boys who verbally abused me and called me gay. I was confused, angry. I didn't fit the stereotypical pupil that bullies usually go for, I thought, and I just didn't know how to fix it. I'd have meltdowns and run away before school. When it happened, it was uncontrollable. I would bolt out of the house, run down roads and hide in people's gardens, in their flowerbeds. Mum would coax me out.

'Please, David, come on. Whatever it is, we can talk about it,' she'd say gently. 'You can't spend all day out here.'

Eventually I'd relent. She'd comfort me and try to get me to talk.

'So long as you speak to me, David, it's okay. Just please don't do this, you know how stressful it is for me. Promise me?'

'I'm sorry, I promise to speak to you.' I would say.

That became our pact.

Eventually the situation came to a head and, as Mum started the school run, I couldn't bear it any more – I simply couldn't go in.

Dad came and stood in the doorway of my bedroom, staring at me as I knelt on the floor with my hands covering my face. He flashed a look at Mum: *this is for you to deal with*, it said.

I tried to go in twice more, each time a disaster. The final time I ran away was the only time my mum ever really reached the end of her tether with me, finally losing her temper. I was stunned – it was so unlike her. But the pressure of trying to fix things for me on her own was too much. I couldn't go back, even for her. Eventually, Mum found me a smaller school.

The smaller school made a big difference, but I did miss my guitar tuition, so I was over the moon when Mum told me she'd organised for Owen, my old guitar teacher, to come to our house for lessons.

But it didn't last. He came to the house a handful of times but he often seemed uncomfortable and, ultimately, wasn't able to commit to the long commute for lessons.

Still I kept grasping at music as a way to connect with Dad. One day, to my surprise, he agreed to visit the music shops of Denmark Street with me, so I could show him my dream guitar: a Sunburst Fender Thinline '72 Telecaster. I had been saving up hard for it and, as I talked him through what made great guitars different from the rest, he was focused on what I was telling him, clearly trying to understand.

'Can't you just replace the pickups in your guitar?'

'No, Dad. I mean, you *can*, but it's the construction of the body, how it plays. It's so much more than just the pickups.'

That Christmas, the exact guitar was waiting for me under the tree. From Dad. I couldn't believe it. He never bought our gifts, and if we needed something we went to Mum. That was how it worked. Our Christmas presents had always been as much a surprise to him as to us, Mum having spent days buying them and carefully wrapping them while preparing everything in the house.

But this he had bought himself. I unzipped the black bag in a state of shock.

He had listened to me. More than the money, it was the unprecedented fact that he had showed a real interest that touched me. For just a moment he was choosing to make me feel worthy of his attention.

*

Such moments were a tantalising glimpse of what could have been. And they were so rare. I was in the process of beginning to understand and explore my sexuality when my internet history was discovered on the family computer. I was so ashamed I hid under the table in the dining room and peered up the stairs towards the office as my mum viewed the 'evidence'.

The next day I hid in the bathroom, refusing to open the door as Mum spoke to me from outside.

'I know, David,' she said 'I know. It's okay.'

I still didn't answer.

'You know, your uncle Brian is gay as well,' she continued in a calm voice.

'Yes, yes, I know,' I stammered.

'Well, I'm here. I'm always here, if you ever need to talk. I will always love you.'

And that was it: I felt safe in my sexuality from that moment on.

I never came out to Dad.

I assumed Mum had told him, but he didn't speak to me about it. Any male friends who came round were given the hard stare.

Several years later, he broached it with me. It was coming up to Christmas, and I was in the kitchen wrapping a present at the table, while he sat there watching television on the wall-mounted set. It was just the two of us. Suddenly, he asked, 'So, are you really gay?'

With no easy way of physically extracting myself from the conversation, I took a deep breath:

'Yes,' I said, 'Yes, Dad, I am.'

'Well, how do you know?'

'I just know,' I said.

'Yes, but how do you know? Have you ever been with a girl?'

'No.'

'So then, how do you know?'

'Trust me, I just know,' I said, with some emphasis.

He left it at that.

And so did I.

By then, I'd grown used to the absence of warmth, and the way small moments could carry an edge had become normal. It was never the words that stayed with me, it was the cold bite behind them. They'd leave marks. He learned to prey on our vulnerabilities. He knew I struggled to make friends, and would use this against me.

On one holiday in Florida we went to an outlet store to buy clothes. As I added a few bargains to the trolley, Dad suddenly took aim.

'Who is that for?' he said, raising an eyebrow. 'You haven't got any friends. Where are you going to wear those?'

I felt the ground swallow me.

He went out of the way to say the words he knew I'd dwell upon.

But it seemed that the quieter I kept, the more the need to stand up to him grew. On one rare occasion when we were watching television together, he started to mimic an Indian person on screen. He put on an exaggerated accent and moved his head side to side in a bigoted pantomime, throwing me a sidelong grin as he did it. He knew I would hate this open racism. He was asking for a reaction.

Instead of asking him to stop, I exploded, as though the lid was being forced from my tightly tamped-down emotions. I had never done that before.

This encouraged his laughter until I was shouting at him. The throttle of my voice kicked into the back of my throat so keenly that I was left rasping.

He stopped, but his smirk revealed his enjoyment: toying with me was a neat pleasure of his. And this was a new level of reaction.

I could feel myself changing. When I witnessed his jibes at Mum, I could see how stoically she was fending him off, refusing to rise to it. And I could see how those defences came at a cost – how she'd shrink just a little bit each time.

At restaurants, I'd watch him grow tense when she reached out to make conversation with people at nearby tables. She'd be mid-sentence, animated and engaged, when his eyes would narrow, his jaw tightening.

'Sally, must you?' he'd mutter, just loud enough to arrest her.

Her response was always the same: a flicker of surprise, a pause, her face folding in slightly as if she'd overstepped some invisible line. Watching that shift in her made something small but sharp twist inside me. Something hard began to take root in me. Resentment, anger and a dull bitterness began to follow me into adulthood.

I started pushing back in quiet ways. Nothing dramatic, just small interjections. Choosing my moments, taking my chances. Changing the subject when his words grew too clipped, steering the conversation away from wherever he was trying to pin her down.

I wasn't trying to fix it. I just couldn't continue to sit there without doing something, no matter how small.

Chapter Six

Mum remained besotted, despite it all. She was always thinking of how best to please him. One birthday, knowing how much he loved cameras, she bought him a Sony mini-DVD video camera, the first of its generation. She told me, as she was wrapping it up, that she had spent all of her bonus and earnings on it: she wanted to get the very best one with all the features.

He shed the wrapping paper with mute disinterest, set the camera aside without taking it out of his its packaging and promptly left the room. The silence was deafening. Mum's eyes locked into the floor.

I knew from my own experience that this was who he was. I'd given him gifts over the years that I had agonised over, just to watch him cast them aside. But this moment, her moment, was brutal to witness. Nothing I could say or do would help.

By my late teens, it emerged that Dad had made a new friend, who came around one night looking like a lizard in a black dinner suit. There was something repugnant about his energy, a malignant force entering our home. Allegedly, this man was going out on a date and wanted to make a good impression, so he'd asked Dad to drop him off in the Ferrari. But that night, Dad didn't return for hours. Other times, he informed Mum that the two of them were off salsa dancing, and that she wasn't allowed to join.

He became more cavalier, going off to do his own thing, not caring about returning Mum's calls or texts. He was beholden to no one. The absence of care, the sharpness tucked into the smallest of moments, it all felt more visible now. I was noticing things I hadn't before. When Mum tried to include him in plans, he'd rebuff them. If she asked him why, there was one line, on repeat: 'Don't question me, Sally'.

I tried to put it all down to him having a mid-life crisis. But nothing was sitting right.

By now, the internet had supplanted Dad's TV habit. Whenever Dad was not at the computer, Mum would jump on it. I followed her into the study one afternoon, and she immediately shushed me, her finger over her lips. 'Look out for him,' she said, moving the mouse around with urgency.

Questions circled in my head:

How long has this been going on for?

What does it mean?

They were questions I didn't really want the answers to. Mum began to text me from upstairs to ask whether Dad was home, so that she could stake out the computer. They were more broken than they appeared.

She pulled me aside one day, asking, 'Do you know anything about your dad going to the London Eye?' Her voice was tight, brittle.

'I found tickets in his coat pocket. I confronted him and he said that I must have put them there.' She held them as if they were evidence, her fingers pressed into the paper as if she was trying to wrench an answer from it.

The fear on her face was worse than the question itself. Something was changing in her, breaking. She had always had a quality of calm and could make the people around her feel better. Now that was gone, and in its place was a terrified panic.

As I returned to my room, Mum's words lingered like a stain. *He said that I must have put them there.* The more I repeated the words, the louder they rang in my head. He expected her to believe that?

What's more, Mum became convinced that a woman had been calling the house. She became less talkative. Her mind seemed elsewhere. It became a routine for her to check his phone. I'd watch her frown whenever she discovered that it was locked with a new pin. Dad was always one step ahead of her, mindful that he was arousing suspicion. Sometimes he'd catch her checking when his phone was on charge.

Mum would try to walk off, then immediately turn back on herself, refusing to accept she was in the wrong.

'Why are you hiding things from me? You're never where you are when you say you are.'

In retaliation, he guarded his mobile more ferociously.

Desperately, Mum began to record everything she had found. Demanding answers, she would lay her evidence out before him.

His response was always the same: 'You're going mad, Sally. You're making it up.'

Over and over again. All the arguments merged into one with no beginning or end.

No, he had nothing to do with the receipt she found for the Prince of Wales theatre on a day he'd told her he was in Germany. He must have picked it up on the sole of his shoe.

No, he had never been to the London Eye.

No, he wasn't calling another woman.

Eventually, when her questioning became too insistent, he snapped.

'You must have put it there yourself,' he said. 'If you keep on, I won't pay for your fare to Australia.'

The trip to Australia was to see Dad's brother John, who was now dying of cancer. It was important to Mum to be able to see him one last time.

It went on for months and months. I would find myself sitting at the top of the stairs, listening to them argue, trying to make sense of the chaos. Searching for the truth, just as Mum was.

'You're making it up.'

'You're making it up.'

'You're making it up.'

I didn't want to get involved.

I felt I had a duty to hear her speak.

I felt I had a duty to remind her that she wasn't going crazy – that she wasn't making it up.

Night after night, all I'd hear was: 'You're going mad, Sally. You're going mad.'

After that, he would say nothing at all.

The house and my head had never been louder.

Chapter Seven

I was 19 now, studying journalism in London and commuting home in the evenings. It was a career choice chosen in small part to please Dad, harking back to his own father's profession. But Mum was the one who gave me all the parental encouragement. She loved to see the articles I wrote for the university paper and the *Gay Times*, where I secured a work placement.

Outside of my studies I struggled to make friends. My circle was small, and being gay only added to this overwhelming sense of loneliness. When I met Ian, a void was filled. We found each other on a gay networking website called Fitlads. net. Neither of us deemed the other 'fit', but what we found was a lasting friendship. Ian was an old head on young shoulders, and we shared the same cynical sense of humour.

One night he stayed the night at mine. The next morning, he sent me a text: 'Do you ever hear about women that play happy families, but are talking to lawyers behind the scenes?' He too had sensed the rot in my house. He never came back.

The arguments continued.

Dad was often out late, allegedly at work. I would find Mum nerving herself up in the kitchen, glass of wine in hand, bolstering the confidence to confront him.

Armed with yet another discovery, she'd begin with

questions. His response was always the same: denial, a refusal to engage, a glassy-eyed stare at the TV.

He wouldn't answer even basic questions. His silence was suffocating, engulfing the whole house and squeezing the air out of every room.

At some point, fortified by a few glasses of wine and total desperation, Mum would start to shout, though this was not her usual character. Questions tumbled out of her in desperation. Where was he, all those times he was not where he said he would be? Was he using the Viagra pills she had found?

His response stayed the same:

'You're going crazy, Sally. You're mad. You're making it all up.'

Or he would employ a new catchphrase, one that burned into my mother's psyche: *Don't question me, Sally. Don't question me.*

Occasionally he would get off the sofa and stand in the doorway of the playroom to use us as some kind of shield. There was a special voice he used in these moments: vulnerable, wheedling and fake. Eventually, burnt out by her frustration, Mum would retreat to the garage and sit in the car, sobbing uncontrollably, blasting out music to calm herself, usually *Patience* by Take That.

Every time I heard that song it bore a hole in my head, knowing she was falling apart, alone.

One evening, Dad beckoned me over from the doorway of the living room, bowing his head to my height until he was speaking right into my ear.

'Look,' he said in a hushed voice, pointing at Mum, who was slouched asleep on the sofa next to a glass of wine. 'Your mother's not well, she's drinking all the time.'

It was like he was trying to display some kind of evidence to me. But I sensed what he was up to. I said nothing.

'You've poisoned my children against me,' he would sometimes say to her in the heat of an argument.

No, you've done that yourself, I would think.

The arguments became so constant that I couldn't bear the sound of them anymore. Hearing the pain in Mum's voice, the constant accusations of madness back from Dad. Playing the guitar was usually the best way to avoid the sound of raised voices, so I'd flick on my amp and turn the volume up.

'You're practising a lot in your room, David,' Mum would say. 'I'm really proud of you, I hope you keep it up.'

I would shrug. She didn't need to know what drove me to practise.

During these years of attrition, Dad became obsessive about the state of the house. It became a wash of greys and creams like a catalogue show home, any vestiges of untidy family life removed. Every surface had to be totally clear and every corner tidy.

Dad would march around the house, finding things to fixate on. He would walk into the kitchen holding a tiny pot that sat in the hallway, lifting out the keys and knick-knacks one by one to interrogate us about their purpose and use. Mum faltered under his questions. I said nothing.

He became possessed by the need to know everything

that was going on, too. He would hide the home telephone, incensed if anyone else used it. All the electrical items in the house – the remote control, the DVD player – were under his control.

Any friends we brought over were treated with suspicion. I stopped bringing people back. What would they think of me, if they knew this is how we lived?

The home began to feel charged with psychological warfare. Ambushes could come from any angle, without warning.

One afternoon, I found Mum sitting on the floor with the phone bills spread out in front of her, going through each entry in exacting detail. Dad had left his phone out the night before, and Mum had taken her chance. In it, she had found a phone number saved as 'Dent Devils'.

'This was the number that kept calling the house,' she said, visibly emotional. 'I phoned the number and a woman answered. I asked if this was Dent Devils and she laughed and said no.'

Her face changed as the words left her mouth, while we sat on the floor together. She looked terrified. It was clear: this was the woman who had been calling. The one Dad had said didn't exist.

Finally: rock solid confirmation.

'I really believed him, you know,' she said. 'I really believed that I was starting to make these things up. I thought it was all in my head. I thought he was telling the truth. Even with the numbers on the phone logs.'

I looked back at her as she crouched on the floor with the

sprawl of his lies laid out in front of her. Her face was tired and worn. We had hit a new abyss.

It wasn't just the cheating, it wasn't just the lying to her face, it was the fact that he had managed to get inside her reality and toy with it until she had become lost in his lies. It was dangerous. It was an attack on her very being. Every time he had brushed her aside or called her mad, he had chipped away at her foundations. And it was also an attack on me. To harm her was to harm me.

An alarm began to sound, and I didn't know what to do about it.

One evening not long afterwards, I was home alone when I heard the front door open and Dad's footsteps. I heard him speak to the cat: 'Hello there, pretty boy. What are you up to?' His voice was high-pitched, forced. Self-conscious.

Something had happened.

Within ten seconds, the front door banged open again. I could hear my mother shouting in full voice: 'I *saw* you, I saw you there. I *saw* you,' over and over.

'What are you talking about? What on earth are you talking about?' Dad replied repeatedly. He seemed to have no other words, like a broken wind-up toy.

I peered down the stairs. Dad was in the hallway, barely moving. Mum was in full tirade: 'You were fucking them. Prostitutes! How long have you been doing this? How long?' she screamed.

I slammed my bedroom door and collapsed to the floor with my back wedged against it. I even braced my feet against the bookcase for good measure, jamming them so hard that the bookshelf teetered and fell against the door above me, barricading me in.

The voices from below – my mother's loud and shrill, my father's quieter and failing – went on for over an hour. Their words bled up the stairs. Tracking a number she had seen in the phone records, a number he had been calling weekly, had led to a brothel called Pandora's. It was behind Surbiton train station, just down the road from Mum's office.

She had driven there that afternoon and waited in a stairwell with a hood up to cover her face. When Dad came out, Mum had intercepted him. I found out later that, caught red-handed, he had looked into her face for a moment, and then ran to his car and driven home as fast as he could.

There it is, I thought. *That's the truth. At last.* Everything that I had been carrying with me, that swirling mist of unease within me, had finally crystallised. That gut feeling, the wrongness I sensed. It had ached away within me for years. Now, here it was. A signal, proven right. But I was shaking. I might have suspected something. I still didn't want it to be true.

Eventually, the voices died down. After my mother had gone to bed, I heard my father's steps coming upstairs and pausing outside my bedroom. I heard him try the handle, not forcefully, but enough of a rattle to let me know he was there.

'David, let me in,' he said in a soft voice.

I said nothing. I pushed my entire weight against the door. I didn't want anything to do with him.

'David, let me in,' he pleaded, his voice calm. He repeated

it a few more times, then 'I'm sorry . . .' When I still didn't respond, I finally heard the soft tread of his footsteps moving down the corridor.

It was thirty minutes or more before I levered my stiff limbs off the floor. I propped my bookcase against the door and got into bed.

For weeks, Dad denied he had been to the brothel. Mum was distraught, refusing to allow him into her bedroom. She felt violated in every single way. Then my uncle Terence and his wife Frances came to visit and, despite Mum's distress, neither she nor Dad wanted them to know they were arguing. Keeping up appearances, Dad would get up early so he wouldn't be found sleeping on the sofa. And each night, Mum confronted Dad again, begging him to admit what he had done. She still clawed for answers. Most of all, she wanted – needed – to know why.

'Just tell me why you did it, why did you go there? Please, Richard. Please.'

Once again, he told her she was mad. This time, Mum had had enough. She poured a glass of water over his head. The house erupted. Hearing the commotion, James and I bolted out of our rooms to find them in a stand-off: Mum incandescent with rage, Dad aghast. All of us trying not to wake our guests.

'Admit it, Dad! Admit it. We know you're lying!' James and I both shouted over and over again, holding Mum behind us to protect her. 'Just admit it! Tell her!' we pleaded.

It was then that he broke.

'Okay, okay, I did it. Okay? I did it.'

Mum slapped him in the face. Dad stood still. A terrible silence broke out.

Finally, I thought.

And then he started crying. I had never seen or heard my dad cry before. It was a noise I could have gone my whole life not hearing. It was too animal, too raw. It was a howl.

We all stood there in the dead of night, paralysed, watching our world crumble before us.

In the days that followed, he wouldn't accept the destruction he had wrought upon us. Instead, he tried out reparations: starting to do things I had never seen him do in his life. He emptied the dishwasher, tried to cook a bit, even went to the supermarket. It was as though an alien had suddenly appeared in the cereal aisle.

But the period of meekness lasted barely a fortnight. Dad grew tired of Mum serving him dinner each night without saying a word. He decided he had suffered enough, and told her that if she continued to be upset, he would leave her: 'Stop this, Sally. What you need to do is move on. Treat this as a bereavement and get over it.'

He even tried to explain it away as a 'man's thing'.

None of his behaviour felt surprising to me any more. I was just resigned. For my mother, though, this was the beginning. The knowledge that he had slept with prostitutes wedged itself deep within her. She suspected that when he had spent a couple of days in Bangkok alone on the way to Australia, it had been for similar reasons. She remembered that he had suddenly added an extra day in Bangkok on another return trip, disappearing from the hotel to have a mysterious 'massage'.

Of course, any enquiries were met with the same refrains:

'You're going mad, Sally.'

'You're imagining it.'

'You need to move on.'

That discovery of Dad's prostitutes blew our world apart. Regardless, within a year he was back to his old ways – skulking on the internet, never being where he said he was, refusing to answer Mum's questions. She became ever more desperate to know.

One afternoon, from the back seat of the car, I watched an argument boil over. Dad had got himself an extra mobile phone. He wouldn't give Mum the number.

She was pleading with him; he was immovable. He wanted his privacy, he said.

Something rose in me: I was bubbling over in frustration. I couldn't sit back and watch this anymore. I was twenty-one now, an adult. As we parked, it burst out of me: 'Why should you have privacy, after all your lying?'

'She's paranoid. She's going through my phone,' he answered.

'It was *you* that made her paranoid. You did that! And she proved she wasn't!' I shot back, unable to understand how he couldn't see this. 'You know why she gets upset. You need to earn back that trust.'

The argument continued to the front door. I walked away from him to my room and he followed, talking and talking at me, facing me down like a power-play. We ended up in my bedroom, standing off against each other, but I was the same height as him now. And I wasn't backing down.

No matter how hard I tried to get through to him, I couldn't make him see it from our point of view.

'She can't hold it over me for ever,' he said, his voice calm. 'People change, and I should be allowed to move on. I deserve my own privacy, I'm not that person any more.'

I blinked, thrown by what he was saying. 'But you *are* that person, dad. You're hiding things, you're doing it again to her now. You've got two phones! This is happening *again*.'

He shook his head, 'Don't be silly, it's for work . . . you're letting her get to you, and you're not helping her, David.'

I felt incensed. I'd had a firm grip on the argument, but somehow it was slipping away. I rallied again.

'Dad, I saw you had been calling that brothel, I heard the lies you told her, night after night. You got caught, you have to earn that trust back. Why don't you see that?'

He stepped closer to me now. A strange smile appeared on his face. It was the same expression he used to have when he'd bested James or me at the mercy-mercy game.

'We all make mistakes. I said sorry, what more do you want?'

My chest tightened. 'You didn't say sorry. You're even smiling about it now.'

He shrugged. 'That's your version.'

Suddenly I realised none of this really meant anything to him. Even though I was armed with every moral argument under the sun, nothing landed on him: he somehow upended every accusation. He was pure Teflon. He took pleasure in the fight. This was all a game, nothing but an opportunity to win. The spoils were our emotional distress.

It began to feel less like an argument and more like I was staging an intervention. I didn't want to *win*, I wanted him to grasp what I was saying. But he couldn't – or wouldn't. And just in that moment, I saw with clarity how maddening and powerful a person my dad was, how a simple discussion with him would detonate your grasp on truth until you began to question basic facts.

It was just a tiny glimpse of what my mother was up against.

Chapter Eight

We took a trip to the Maldives. We went diving off boats, rigged up in masks and flippers. The drop into the sea always terrified Mum. 'Grab my hand!' I would say as she bobbed up to the surface. Her hair would get helplessly caught in her goggles, and I would have to adjust them for her as she spat and spluttered in a panic.

'Mum, it's okay. Just keep swimming.'

I shared her fear of the deep water, but the reef was also my haven. We trundled up and down together, pointing out the marvellous wonders we spotted: clouds of multicoloured creatures; odd-looking Napoleon fish with big turquoise heads; and once even a green turtle being gently swept along by the current. I loved those moments – just the two of us, the underwater groves of coral an echo of the wooded solitude from my early childhood, years before.

But tensions that evaporated in daylight started to pool back into the early evening shadows. Mum leaped at the opportunity to be social on holiday, flashing smiles to fellow guests and giving them a compliment or regaling them with an anecdote. James and I tended to recede in embarrassment at this, while Dad would sigh and stay silent as long as possible, as Mum pined for interaction.

On the final evening, a local DJ played in the bar. I watched with a horrible sense of premonition as couples started to dance. Mum's eyes were fixed on the moving bodies, her spine beginning to sway to the music, fingers and feet tapping. Dad, meanwhile, was staring straight ahead. She leapt up, and tried to persuade him onto the dance floor. No dice: Dad was planted solid. *Just give her one or two songs,* I willed him.

I could measure the beats of each moment, having witnessed this kind of scene play out countless times at parties – Mum dancing, smiling and cajoling him as he sat motionless, blank eyes boring into hers, demanding she sit back down.

Unable to bear it, I went back to my room. The evening had soured, and any hope that this break might dispel the tension had been extinguished.

Later that night, James and I were woken by Mum suddenly bursting into our room, jolting us out of sleep. Something about her was frighteningly off-kilter.

'What's going on? What's happened?' I asked.

'It's . . . he . . . your father wouldn't dance with me. Do you remember?'

We nodded.

'Well, we started to argue about it . . .' She stopped, and seemed to have to make an effort to continue. 'And then suddenly . . . he was pushing me back to the room. Trying to stop me from arguing with him. And when we got there, he grabbed me . . . I was screaming, and he . . . he was trying to cover my mouth. To shut me up.'

Through everything else we had witnessed over the years, we had not ever seen him lay his hands on her. This time I felt no confusion, just pure fury. There was something different about Mum. She looked stunned and appalled, but measured.

'What are you going to do?' I asked.

'I'm divorcing him. I can't take it any more. I can't do it. His lying, his cheating. That's it, I'm sorry.'

Inside I cheered, proud that she was making a decision for herself at last, and not for him.

Finally, we would all be free.

The next morning was filled with silence as we packed our bags. Mum tried to put on a brave face as she herded us through the baking hot airport. Memories of LA swirled in my head. Except this time, Mum was doing the herding, not Dad.

As we waited to board, just as though nothing had happened yesterday, Dad set off on a familiar riff about his hatred of mobile phones and his desire to buy some piece of tech that could apparently jam other people's signals. We held our tongues. We had heard all this before. I shifted in my chair, trying to catch James's eye. But our silence didn't stop Dad. On he went. He chatted incessantly. He was trying to provoke a reaction, a mischievous grin on his face the whole time.

I looked at him then, and I realised: we were nothing but a sideshow to him. It was clear that he didn't even really see us as his family any more. At some point in the past decade, that sense of family had been extinguished, and what we were seeing now were the cold, dying embers.

Chapter Nine

Nothing came of Mum's desire to divorce for some time. She went back on mute.

I felt myself slipping away too. I was confused and lost. The walls had an endless shudder to them now, as if stuck in shockwave.

Mum and Dad were scheduled to head up north to see friends in Scotland, but my depression had worsened until I was at crisis point. Worried about me, Mum decided I should come too, and sat with me in the back of the car for the journey.

Struggling through my anguish as Dad drove, I felt my body being jerked ferociously around and realised he was driving increasingly erratically, braking so hard at one point that Mum hit her head on the passenger seat in front.

'Richard, what are you doing?' she said. No answer.

'Can we pull in at the next service station?' she asked a little later. We watched as Dad sailed past the next exit.

Eventually he stopped and allowed us to go to the bathroom. As we returned to the car, I could see he hadn't moved. He was still, stoically holding his hands on the wheel and looking dead ahead. *This is going to escalate.*

He wouldn't start the car.

'Richard, what's wrong?' Mum asked, genuinely concerned about him. No answer.

She asked him again, several times over. Still no response. The car became suffocating, as though all the air was vacuumed out. Mum and I looked at each other, my rising sense of panic reflected in her eyes. Finally, he answered.

'Sally. You're criticising my driving and it's not acceptable. I think we should turn around and head back.'

'Turn around and go home?' Mum asked. 'Why? You can't be serious?'

'I'm afraid I am,' he said, his tone resolute. Then he sat.

A pause stretched out until my nerves were taut as a high wire. Then: 'I'm sorry. I'm sorry I criticised your driving. I'm sorry,' Mum pleaded. 'I won't say anything about your driving again. Please, Richard, please. We all need this trip. David needs this trip.'

It must have been what he was waiting for. He put the car into gear and drove. I was in the back now, racking my brains as to what had just happened.

Dad didn't seem to like it when Mum paid too much attention to my problems. *That was it,* I thought. *I wasn't meant to be on this trip, and now I am.* He wanted her to apologise, focus only on him.

Mum found me a counsellor, telling me to see her as much as I needed.

Dad never acknowledged my therapy until one day when I returned from a session and was sitting in the living room, trying to get my head together. He was loitering in the doorway. His presence bore down on me; he wanted to make a point. 'How's the therapy going?' he asked.

'Okay,' I replied. I really didn't want to talk about it.

He peered out the window, took a sip of his coffee and paused once more. 'You know each time you go there it costs your mother money?'

He stood silent for a while, a silhouette against the light, until he was sure that the weight of his words had sunk onto my shoulders.

I always felt guilty taking any money from Mum, knowing that ever since she had started working full time her money was increasingly being used for all the things that Dad had stopped paying for, like our food. But I'd never borrow so much as a fiver from Dad – he would immediately make you feel lacerating guilt about it. If you wanted something, you would go to Mum. If you wanted something from Dad, you'd still submit your proposal to Mum, and she would negotiate on your behalf behind closed doors.

I said that I didn't need the therapy any more.

One night my parents were watching TV together when a news segment came on, an exposé on trafficked women. They reported a raid on a brothel: Pandora's.

Everything my mother had been trying to bury in the face of Dad's stonewalling came rearing with a lurch to the surface. The humiliation, the disgust. She called the police.

Sitting at the top of the stairs, I could hear her voice, tense and erratic as she told the operator she had information that could help convict those involved in the brothel, 'because my husband is one of the parties involved.'

There was a pause as the operator said something. And then things got weird.

'No,' she snapped flatly, 'he's dead.'

'I'm a stressed wife,' she added a minute or two later, 'and please don't push me.'

I could hear her unravelling. I put my head in my hands and listened hopelessly to Mum's back and forth with the operator, until she handed the phone to Dad.

Speaking into the receiver, Dad sounded worried and slightly tremulous as he thanked the operator for her concern. 'It's okay. My wife's had too much to drink,' he said.

It wasn't just the words; it was the delivery. He knew how to play the victim. Soon enough, blue lights shone hotly into our house. The officers were downstairs talking to Mum and Dad, trying to make sense of what was going on. The call-out was chalked up as drunken behaviour, and after a quick follow-up visit a day or two later, we were left alone. On neither visit did the police speak to my mother alone. Nor did they ask to speak to me.

As I had seen from the stairs that evening, it was clear there was no turning back for Mum. I knew as I saw her peer with horror at the screen, images from the brothel engulfing her. For years, Dad had kept the truth welded in behind a locked door. But we all knew there was something wrong. We were just waiting for him to make a mistake so that we could see what was behind the door.

When Mum found him at the brothel, she had tried to seal the door back up. But the truth had been leaking into her mind ever since. She wanted to stay with him. But to do that she needed the truth. The TV exposé was the start of three to four weeks of endless arguments, her desperate pleading to find out why he went to the brothel, what more he was hiding from her. She begged for an amnesty.

'Tell me the truth, Richard!' she pleaded. 'I need to know – you have to tell me. You know that, right? There's more, I know there is, and I have a right to hear it.'

But Dad simply locked himself within his body, utterly silent. Occasionally, he would come up for air to repeat yet more mantras:

'*I've told you before, Sally. Treat it as a bereavement – you must try.*'

'*It's a man's thing, Sally. Now move on.*'

Once again, the campaign of arguments rolled on day after day, reverberating throughout the home, ringing in my head. I would retreat upstairs as soon as I'd finished dinner, giving her an encouraging nod as I made myself scarce.

After the TV exposé on Pandora's though, Mum's manner was different, she was determined. It felt like a final push.

And then finally she reached the end.

Chapter Ten

Mum was leaving. The roles reversed.

'You can't take the business, that's mine! I worked for that.' Dad was furious.

At the top of the stairs I could see Mum: focused, determined, blinkers on to protect her from the extremity of emotion. Nothing was going to distract her. Below, Dad was clinging onto the bannisters and peering upwards with a look of desperation on his face.

For a moment I was caught between them. But, looking back up at Mum, a wave of pride passed over me. She was finally going to be free.

'Please – just tell me what you want,' Dad would plead, desperate to get Mum's attention. Mum refused to acknowledge him, the silence he had meted out to her for decades returned to him in spades.

He was worried that she might lay claim to the business. In his eyes, because he had created it, he alone had any kind of right to it. The years of support she had given him – the help with his accounts, the picking up of vehicles, the shouldering of every domestic burden to allow him the freedom to work – counted for nothing to him.

He also felt that a man should have a family at home, somebody to come back to after his Ferrari owners' trips. Someone to call when he was away. We were part of the package that came with being a successful man: nice home, nice clothes, nice car, nice family. Mum had done everything for him, and he was about to lose all that too.

She moved fast. She had come into an inheritance when Granny Jenney died, which allowed her a degree of freedom. One evening I came home to find her sitting at the kitchen table. She beckoned me over, opening a folder filled with house listings, all neatly collated together in separate sleeves.

'I want you to tell me which one you want to live in.'

In that moment, I realised what the divorce meant for me. There was no question about who would get the house. Dad would claim it, just like every other object in our lives. The home was paid for by him, as he liked to remind us. To him, it wasn't our family home, it was just his. I would, of course, go with Mum, Pepe the dog would come with us too, but Mum's beloved cat Tiggy was too old to uproot, and would stay with Dad. James was determined to stay, but in reality he was spending more and more time with his partner, Jen. Our family was over. This feeling of severance stayed with me as I looked through page after page of houses that were not home.

The house at Ruxley Ridge was all I had ever known. It wasn't the easiest place to live, but it was the only home I knew.

Mum left me to it, but it didn't take me long. 'This one,' I said when she returned, pointing to a detached three-bedroomed new-build in a small gated community called Ashton Place. 'This one looks nice. Modern. Kind of comfortable.'

I was lying. I picked it because it was the closest to Ruxley Ridge, only a 15-minute walk away. *If I can't stay at home, I'll stay as close as I possibly can,* I reasoned, clinging onto familiarity as the bedrock of my life turned to sand.

I still wake up in the middle of night, wishing I had gone through that folder more carefully. It felt as though no sooner had I pointed out the house than Mum and I were standing outside it. It was considerably smaller than Ruxley Ridge.

This will be my new home.

We spent a couple of nights in Ashton Place, bending ourselves awkwardly to fit into our new home, trying to pretend everything felt natural. Just the two of us.

We returned to the old house to collect the last of our stuff. I could sense Dad was home as soon as we walked through the door, even before I caught sight of him at his usual spot in front of the TV. He made no acknowledgement that we were leaving, going about his life as though we were already gone. I scuttled about the house, desperate to be as quick as possible. It felt weirdly illicit, as though I didn't belong any more, in the only home I had ever known.

Noel and Mum waited for me in the kitchen. Noel had helped Mum with furnishing Ashton Place, as it had been made abundantly clear that she would not be allowed to take much from Ruxley Ridge. It was odd that her part of the house, the kitchen, was now his domain. She wasn't taking a lot, just Granny Jenney's cooking knife along with a few pots and pans. Mum looked weathered, as though she was losing her place in the world.

I was on my knees in the playroom, filling a storage box with games and mementoes. As I picked up the detritus of my childhood, it was as though the memories stored in them became an uprush of emotion spilling out in tears. And with them came a fury. Our family was dividing itself at the root, and Dad was just sitting in front of the TV. I was overcome. *He doesn't care. He doesn't care.* Tears streamed down my face. Before I knew what I was doing, I had pushed the box over and stood up.

Mum and Noel heard the commotion and came after me, but it was too late. I was now towering in front of my seated father.

'What are you doing? WHAT ARE YOU DOING?! You don't even care. After all your cheating. After all you did to Mum. You think you have a God-given right to do what you want. Fuck other women, have affairs, make Mum question herself. You're a fucking cunt and I hate you. I hate you!'

I let out every sentence I had been replaying for years over and over in my head, never dreaming I would say any of it to his face. It was one violent expulsion.

Dad sat open-mouthed as his eyes flitted from me to Mum and back again in an exaggerated gesture. Mum and Noel stood in the living room doorway. Neither of them spoke.

I took a deep breath and looked down on him, small in his seat. That's it, I thought. I'm done with him.

I could hear Mum behind me as I left, making excuses to Dad. 'He's just emotional,' she said.

Chapter Eleven

'*Chop . . . chop . . . chop . . .*'

The metronome of Granny Jenney's knife hitting a chopping board reverberated through the thin walls of the house, stirring me awake and reminding me I was no longer at home, with him.

A physical wave of relief washed over my body, and everything that had seized up inside of me over the years shifted. I no longer needed to safeguard Mum. There was nobody to tell her what to do, to pressure her into servitude. I headed downstairs to embrace this new-found freedom in Mum's presence. The kitchen felt strange, all hard and hostile surfaces. The home was clean and perfectly set out, but somehow lifeless. It felt precarious. We were safe but fragile.

Of course it isn't going to feel homely yet, I told myself. I didn't want to grieve the familiarity of the old house – I wanted to only see the new.

Mum saw something of this on my face.

'The kitchen's a lot smaller than Ruxley, but I've got everything I need,' she offered. It hurt to see her try so hard.

I nodded, doing my best to mirror her encouragement. 'It's great. We don't need much.'

'I'll find some nice garden chairs to put outside,' she said. The sentences seemed to hang and wither in the air, her face falling as she spoke. We were both playing our parts in those first few days, but sometimes I would catch her staring vacantly down at her plate or out of the window, and wonder what she was thinking.

A few months later, it was Christmas. And it was desolate.

James and Jen visited from Essex, where James was spending most of his time. He was meant to be based at the old house, but Dad had shut off the heating packages. Ashton Place, meanwhile, offered him a room the size of a cupboard.

Mum tried her utmost to transplant Christmas. She cooked a Christmas lunch with all the trimmings: turkey, bread sauce, gravy, greens. A Ruxley Ridge Christmas had involved Mum doing all the work to produce a picture-perfect Christmas for us, wrapping every present three days in advance, loading our stockings with goodies, producing endless appetisers and drinks, until the crowning moment of the Christmas dinner itself, when Dad would stand with great ceremony at the head of the table and carve – his only job.

Now it was just the four of us, trying to ignore the sadness that hovered over the small pine-wood dining table in the living room. I could see James and Jen were concerned by Mum. They too noticed that her early stoicism was slipping.

'I'm sorry I don't have all the things you're used to having, I tried to get everything,' she said with her head down, folding and unfolding her mouth.

'It's fine!' we rushed to reply, falling over each other's voices in our haste to reassure her.

It wasn't the same, though. We all knew that. Dad was

spending Christmas elsewhere, with neighbours apparently. We didn't talk about it, but I couldn't help but sense James was occupied with his worries about him too.

Dad and I were now existing in separate universes. He had emailed me not long after we moved out, giving me his side of the story. He said that blaming him for the divorce may make Mum and me 'feel better', but that it was 'destructive and fuelled further resentment'. He cited the forty years and the 'happy times' they'd had in their marriage together, but said that he couldn't change the past.

His words weren't quite the whole story, though. I knew from James that Dad was blaming Mum for the end of their marriage. His newly adopted stance was that his life was private from us now. Women he was seeing, or who he might take back to our family home, weren't our business.

I had replied, reminding him of the repugnant guilt he had laid on me for having therapy. I told him that I remembered how he used to tell me to 'be a man' and to 'own up to things'. I wanted him to take his own advice.

I told him I remembered all the arguments over the years, and every time he had told mum that she was 'delusional', and 'going insane'. And, finally, that he had almost managed it – he *had* almost driven our mother insane.

But I also knew there were ties with him that I couldn't cut. I had graduated from my journalism course now, and with every job I applied for I knew there was something in me that was trying to prove myself to Dad. Part of me was doing it for him, not me. Why?

*

After Christmas, things got worse. It felt like Mum wasn't just stuck any more; she was regressing. She spent more and more time on the phone to friends, chain-smoking, with Pepe perched on her knee.

She would buttonhole anyone she could, telling them how much she missed Dad. Her face was permanently glued to the phone, speaking day and night to anyone willing to listen to her talk about him. I would try to get her attention, but it was as if she was waiting on hold on a helpline.

'I don't have the will to make the garden nice here. I loved my garden at home . . . Maybe I should just go back?'

'He's being stubborn, not answering the divorce lawyer's emails, switching divorce lawyers.'

'Noel said she's going to wash her hands of me if I keep talking about your father.'

She had started to look a lot thinner, and I'd noticed she was eating far less.

'I'm bored,' she would constantly say. She didn't know what to do. Who to be without his direction.

'What should I do, David?' she asked, slumped in the kitchen.

I had no real answers.

'You need to find a hobby or something to keep you busy, Mum.'

'I don't know,' she replied despondently. 'Maybe I'd be better jumping off Beachy Head'

'Mum!' I said, horrified she would pass that off as a throwaway comment.

She may have physically torn herself away from the old house, but a huge part of her identity remained there. She had lived her entire adult life in service to Dad's needs. She didn't know how to comport herself without his structure and schedule. For so many decades, every single thing she did revolved around him. Now it was as if the beat she had danced to for her entire life had abruptly stopped, and the silence and irregularity of freedom were deafening her.

She wasn't easy to live with. Nor was I. We were both trying to survive. I told myself that things would get better in time. She was in the grieving stage, but she was out of that marriage. That was the main thing.

Perhaps I didn't want to interrogate it too much. I had been worried about her for so long, and now it was time to live my own life.

Also, I had finally met someone: Anthony.

We met on the internet, then discovered we had both previously studied at the same place. Then months later, in Embankment one snowy festive evening, it was as easy to talk in person as online. Before long, we were in a relationship.

One evening we were at the house in Ashton Place, trying and failing to find a movie to watch.

'There's loads over at the old house,' I said. 'Let's just go round and get them.'

Walking to Ruxley Ridge felt weird, but strangely good. Part of me wanted to show Anthony the scene of my childhood memories. Slotting the house key into the front door, I unlocked it just as I had a thousand times before.

Immediately I was hit by the force of the smell inside: Dad's scent, so familiar but somehow magnified to an overwhelming degree. The hair rose on my arms. The house was dark and cold, and though the furniture and layout were all the same, it felt much changed.

We crept in quietly, and I pointed Anthony to the quiet spots on the stairway so the treads wouldn't creak.

'*This was my home too, this was my home too,*' I kept thinking.

I opened the door to my brother's room, freezing as I heard a call from below.

'Who's there?!'

'It's me, Dad. It's David. I'm just getting some DVDs from James's room.'

'You really should let me know before you come round,' he shot back, the tone of his voice whisking me straight back to childhood.

I couldn't tell exactly where in the house his voice was coming from. The old, familiar echoes of the place were distorted, as though the house itself was rejecting me. 'That's my dad,' I mouthed to Anthony. His eyebrows shot up in shock at the coldness of it all.

After that, I didn't have any contact with Dad for quite a while – until I turned on my computer one day to find an email from him with the subject line 'TIGGY'.

I clicked on it with my breath held.

'Oh my God, oh my GOD, *MUM* !' I shouted.

The email was curt: he was sorry, he said, but the cat had been really ill, and he'd had it put down.

I was unable to believe what I was reading. He had him put down, without speaking to us at all? Without giving us the chance to be part of the decision? Or even to say goodbye? Dad always had something left in his arsenal.

Worst of all, Mum loved that cat. Part of me worried that he had not got in touch with her about this deliberately, to get her attention, or even to hurt her. If so, it worked.

She darted for her car keys and wanted to drive to Ruxley Ridge immediately.

'Is that a good idea?' After my last experience, I didn't want to go anywhere near Dad. It felt different now, dangerous even. The idea of him speaking to her scared me. But I couldn't find the words to tell her.

Once we arrived, the familiar red brick façade loomed over me. The garden, the trees, the white windows and doors like a child's doll's house. I couldn't go inside.

'You go in without me,' I said, expecting her to be in there for a couple of minutes, a quarter of an hour at most.

As the minutes passed, I grew uneasy. I looked at my phone – she'd been in there fifteen minutes already. She couldn't be much longer, surely? But time kept ticking by. Half an hour. Forty-five minutes. By now, a feeling of doom was prickling up and down my spine. *It's too long. It's too long. Why is she taking so long? What is she doing in there?*

I knew that the more prolonged the contact she had with him, the more opportunity he would have to pierce her resolve. Just as I was making my mind up to go inside, the door opened.

'What happened?' I asked her.

'Nothing, he just said the cat was unwell.'

'That's it?!'

She didn't respond. She was still mentally engaged in

another conversation. I sat back as my uneasiness doubled. She was hiding something.

At breakfast a few weeks later, she began to talk to me with a nervous expression on her face. 'I want to talk about your father,' she started. 'He's agreed to accept me back if I sign this post-nuptial agreement.'

She delivered this news in the same register she had just used to ask me to pass her the milk.

What?

I took a deep breath, 'What do you mean, post-nuptial agreement?'

'If he's going to get back with me, I would have to follow some rules he's set out. He sent an email.'

'What rules?' I asked, trying to stay even-toned.

She produced a piece of paper.

I will consider your return only on these terms, Mum read, without any shock in her voice.

You will continue and complete the divorce with a £200,000 settlement.

When we go out together it means that: together. This constant talking to strangers is rude and inconsiderate.

We'll agree to items in the home together.

To give up smoking.

To give up your constant interruptions when I am speaking.

I stared at her in amazement. What in the hell was he *thinking*? What in the hell was *she* thinking?

'What do you think?' she said.

WHAT DID I THINK?

It was a land grab. A way of seeking total control over her, making her utterly subservient to him. In signing this she would lock herself up forever. He could treat her as he liked after that, and she would have no recourse. I didn't know a great deal about divorce law, but I had a pretty good idea that £200,000 was a lot less than she would be entitled to after 31 years of marriage to Dad.

All her hard-won freedom, gone. Gone just like that.

'You'd be mad to sign that, Mum,' I said. 'Do *not* sign it, please. I'm begging you.'

'Okay,' she answered without arguing, her voice still neutral.

She didn't bring it up again, so I thought she had seen the light. I was wrong. Her silence on the subject meant something else entirely.

Some time later, Anthony and I were at the cinema in Kingston. As we waited in the queue, I saw a man standing nearby. As his profile came into view, a shot of adrenaline ran through me.

'Jesus! That's my dad,' I said to Anthony. I was taken over by a visceral need not to be seen. He went back to stand in the queue without seeing me, and then I saw a blonde woman next to him. The jangling in my nerves lasted throughout the film.

I felt dirty when I got home that night. It was clear that he had been waiting for someone. Here Mum was, telling everyone how much she missed him, and there he was, out on a date. I felt I had to tell Mum. Catching her in the hallway when I got home, I delivered the news in haste.

'Mum, I was at the cinema with Anthony and I saw him.'

'Who?' she asked.

'Dad. And he was with someone. Like it was a date,' I said.

She took it in with a look of deliberate stoicism.

'Thank you for telling me,' she said.

That was it. I hoped she had taken it on board.

I was to see him one last time.

It was 1 April, my birthday. I was alone in the house when I heard the letterbox clang. I looked out of the window and there, on the front step, was Dad. His face was so out of place at the new house that I questioned my eyesight. He must have climbed over the community gate. He glanced upwards briefly, but he didn't see me and I didn't call down.

I went slowly downstairs and picked the envelope off the mat. It had my name on it. I had to nerve myself to open it. When I did there was a birthday card inside. A generic birthday card with a generic birthday message, nothing personal. The more I looked at the white space and the sparse print, the less I understood. The guy had scaled a gate to post this to me, but had nothing to say. Not even after six months with no calls, no texts, no attempt to check in. He hadn't even rung the doorbell.

It summed up our relationship. An empty-hearted token.

The strange image lingered: Dad standing outside our new house, foreshortened by the angle as he glanced around this unfamiliar territory. He looked powerless. It stayed in my mind long afterwards.

Chapter Twelve

The English summer was threatening a heatwave. The trees were sweltering under the pressure of the rising heat, trying to survive into the coming autumn.

Mum had declined even further. I was planning to move to Brighton to study at university. I was less worried about how I would cope and more about how Mum would. I felt guilty for leaving her.

As my leaving day grew closer, distracted by everything I needed to sort out, I saw less of her. She wasn't in the house as often as she had been. She seemed to always be off out, doing something.

When I did see her, her expression was vacant. One morning I heard the tap running, chairs being moved about. She was home. I went down to have breakfast with her in the kitchen.

Mum was standing at the kitchen sink behind me, washing up the bowls and mugs. She wasn't responding to what I was saying, so I threw in a question or two.

'I just don't want to be too far out from campus and everything, you know? Maybe I should get a bike. Do you think I should get a bike?'

Nothing. The conversation started to feel more like a monologue.

'Mum?'

Still nothing.

I turned to look at her. She was staring vacantly down the sink, scrubbing away. Lost in her own unreachable world.

'Mum?'

'Yes, yes? Sorry, what were you saying?' The words flurrying out of her.

'A bike. I was asking whether I should get one?'

'Oh, well . . . I suppose so,' she said, slowly returning to her surroundings. She rolled up her sleeve to check the time. 'What time do you need to leave?'

She was on autopilot.

A few days later everything changed. She was incredibly energetic, positive, her once-felled body now upright and at full attention.

I realised what was going on before she said it. All those days she was out. Fridays were her day off.

She was seeing Dad, every Friday.

That positive mood evaporated as quickly as it had arrived. She was barely around, and when I did see her, her mind seemed to be floating elsewhere.

One day at the beginning of August I was on the way to the train station with Anthony. I called Mum, asking if she had seen my favourite T-shirt.

As soon as she picked up, I could tell something was off. There was total silence on the line.

'Mum,' I repeated, 'are you there?'

She didn't answer. And then she hung up the phone. It was entirely out of character.

I stared at the phone in my hand for a moment. And then

I realised exactly where she was. I knew those acoustics, that particular echo, that reverberation: she was in our old kitchen in Ruxley Ridge. Without hesitation, I dialled again.

'You're in the kitchen at Ruxley, aren't you?' I said.

She didn't answer.

'What are you doing there?' I asked, and again she stonewalled me.

I asked again: 'Why are you there? You shouldn't be there.'

Suddenly, she started crying. 'Leave me alone,' she whimpered, and hung up.

Every siren in my head blared. Fridays were the days she saw Dad, in secret. She had no reason in the world to be there at lunchtime on a Wednesday. And I had a horrible suspicion that this wasn't the first time. What was she up to?

It felt like things were snowballing, that I was missing something important. I had the uneasy suspicion that I was being left out of a loop I hadn't even known existed. I was right.

'How would you feel if me and your father got back together?' she asked me out of the blue one evening.

I could tell from her manner that she had informed everyone but me.

'We're going to live in Australia for bit,' she explained. 'Sell Ruxley and then come back to live at Ashton Place together.'

I felt nothing but exhaustion. I wasn't angry, not really. I knew she was tired. I'd seen the strength she once had – the woman who'd marched upstairs, ignored his calls, stood firm as she moved out. But that strength was now threadbare.

I wanted to fight it, to shake her out of it, but what was the point? He'd already won. His claws were back in, and she looked . . . happy. That was the hardest part. I couldn't take that from her. I just sat with it, swallowed it, knowing I'd be off to university soon, drifting further from both of them. We were both adrift, really. Two people who once lit up around each other, now flickering like two ships far apart on the horizon.

I told myself there was nothing I could do, but maybe that was just easier than admitting I didn't know how.

'I won't live with him again, Mum. Not after everything he's done to you and us.'

But telling me was a formality she had to go through. She was not seeking approval. Nothing I could say would make a difference. I was sidelined.

Chapter Thirteen

I wish I had paid more attention. I wish I had realised how lost she really was. That her absence wasn't just an absence from me, but a parting of ways with herself.

It would be years – decades – before I would understand exactly what had begun to take place, what had been put into motion between them without our knowledge. My father wasn't offering her a life raft. He was beckoning her onto the rocks. She had tried to swim alone and had come to the realisation that sooner or later she would drown. He had used her fear in the face of the unknown to lure her back, and I hated him for it.

Because things had been worse, much worse, than I had thought.

She had spent the months after Christmas plotting her suicide.

She'd travelled to a bridge on the M25 and, of course, to Beachy Head.

In her desperation, she had started messaging Dad, begging him to take her back. '*I want to be with you. I am sorry I left. We are soulmates. I can't see a future without you. You are my life, I love you,*' she had written.

Dad had offered the Friday meetings as a test. He told her they could see each other once a week to see if she had changed. She had to prove herself to him.

She ignored the advice of everyone who told her that going back to him would destroy her. She heard it from friends, from family, from colleagues. Her divorce lawyers told her point-blank that it would be a mistake and she had still told them to go ahead to agree to his offer. Even a friend of Dad's had told her: 'Don't go back with him, he will ruin your life.'

She wouldn't hear any it.

Instead, she distanced herself from everyone until her isolation closed in. She knew that what she wanted was wrong but saw no other way to survive, and so she became secretive. She had no one left to confide in. She was alone in her fight with and for him. A perfect silent hostage.

And around the edges of her resolve crept in the old suspicions, the worries. Was this all a ruse for him to pay her less money, to trap her? He told her that he wouldn't give up his new friends – friends she knew were women he had met on dating sites. She wondered if he was once again seeing prostitutes. The old desperation for the truth kicked back into gear. She started to track his movements obsessively, researching the people he was seeing and doing everything she could to find out what he was hiding from her. Trying to ensure that his agreement to get back together still held water.

As they started to clear the house at Ruxley Ridge together, ready for the idyllic trip to Australia, she noticed that he seemed to be palming useless stuff on to her to store at Ashton Place, keeping the rest himself. He wouldn't answer her at all when she tried to speak to him about money worries. She began to think that he was setting her up, that he would have her sign the agreement and then go off without her, free of her claim on his business and with the belongings he wanted, leaving her with the useless leftovers of their life together.

Her mind began to split – as she concealed her panic and dreams from everyone. She only thought of him and what he could do to her and what he had promised her. Half of her was desperately grasping for the promise of her old life back with him, the other drowning in anguish because she knew he was setting her up for a fall.

On Saturday 14 August, she went back once more to Ruxley Ridge to continue clearing the house.

And then the words: *Don't question me, Sally, don't question me.*

She picked up the hammer, and the force with which she brought it down broke the shape and form of all our lives.

AFTERMATH

Chapter One

'They've got her, she's safe.'

It was the policeman speaking. She had been talked down from the precipice at Beachy Head.

But 'safe' meant something else to them. She was 'safe' in police custody: safely handcuffed and in a van on the way to a cell. To be stored in some faraway place, alone but contained.

As this new reality congealed into a waking nightmare, the blue uniforms before me were quickly replaced by smart-looking suits.

Two FLOs – police Family Liaison Officers – had arrived at Noel's house.

Sarah, with brown hair and glasses, was clearly the lead. Maxine, taller and blonde, stood close behind.

'David, our role is to support you through this. Let us know if you need anything at all – we're here to keep you informed and help you in any way possible,' said Sarah.

I got up to shake their hands and collapsed back into the folds of the sofa. They appeared concerned, but as they asked me to describe my last sighting of Mum earlier that morning, I realised that I was now involved in an 'investigation'. I began to worry that they weren't here to help us as much as I'd hoped; I didn't know what I should or shouldn't say. I wasn't just a victim; I was a witness.

After a few hours, I was told I could speak to my mother.

As the FLO handed the phone to me, muffled, chaotic-sounding noises rattled down the earpiece, transporting me to where she was: a pit of despair. I pressed my ear tighter to the earpiece. I felt rudderless.

'Hello, hello?' her tangled-up voice called out across the line.

'Yes. Yes . . . I'm here, Mum. I'm here.' The right words seemed impossible to find. Her voice was thick with the fug of shock, as though she had just climbed out of a car wreck.

Are you all right?

Are you all right?

We asked each other over and over again.

The hours receded and the darkness of the evening drew in. I waited in the living room until finally the lights of James's car headlights swung through the gaps in the curtains as he pulled into the driveway. I didn't wait for him to clear the corridor – even before he had put down his bags I was running to hug him, feeling my own numbness reflected back at me. Jen followed him into the house, and to my astonishment she had Pepe the dog with her.

'How did you get him?!' I asked. I had been imagining Ashton Place cordoned off by police.

'The police allowed us to call out to him and he came.'

It was a tiny glimmer of comfort.

By the next day, more voices had entered the house. James and Jen had been joined by my uncles and cousin. They were sitting round the garden table outside, planning legal steps. The FLOs were overseeing everything, just within earshot.

'We can't trust them completely,' I said as quietly as I could to my brother, flicking my eyes towards them.

'Why?' James asked

'They're still police,' I replied.

'Oh,' said James, the reality of our situation landing on him with a dull thud.

We looked at each other as they handed us pens and statement forms, then sat, metres apart, staring into space as we tried to give them some words. I raised my head from the page to check something with James, and then became aware of the presence of the FLOs. I lapsed back into silence.

It must have been after lunch that Sarah came to us and in a sombre voice explained that one of us would have to identify our father's body.

I volunteered immediately. It was instinctive and equally considered.

I needed to see Dad one last time. To understand what had happened to him. What Mum had done. I needed to look him in the face, because from the instant I knew she had killed him my instinct had been that he was the architect of everything that had led to this moment. I knew that whatever had driven her to do it had been created within her by him. I knew that in my gut. But I knew I also had to understand the full impact of what Mum had done to him. I needed to understand what he had gone through. I owed him that.

From the back of the car, I watched the outside world pass by on our way to the mortuary. How was it all still moving, unaware of this seismic shift? I was no longer part of it. I was trapped in the grotesque.

I walked through the mortuary's doors into a waiting area. It was medical and clinical, with its white-washed walls and plastic chairs. I waited in silence. Then a small woman appeared. She was older than all of us, but she moved swiftly, never making eye contact. She pushed a glass of water towards me and ordered me to drink it. She knew how to handle people in these moments. I felt like a piece of aeroplane wreckage, being carefully handled by a forensic team.

'Now, what will happen is I'll open the door and you'll go in. It will be dark, but there will be a light on him. Take your time to look at him and then come back out.'

She pulled open the big, vault-like door.

The gurney was angled upwards. A light was trained on the body that lay on it. The moment took on the texture of a nightmare: walking through a dark room to where a light shone on a person who was no longer there.

Again, reality warred with memory. Yes, this was my father, but not my father. He had shaved his goatee and his face was stripped of its sardonic expression. Aside from the bandages around his head, he could have been asleep. But there was a quiet violence in the stillness of his body, the total absence of life.

I had thought that in this goodbye, I might find meaning at last. He was my dad, and I his son. Deep in my bones, I still felt those early memories of me curled up on the sofa next to him, falling asleep cradled in his arms and love.

However he had treated Mum, had treated us, he didn't deserve this.

I was ushered out. The woman gave me another glass of water before looking at me expectantly.

Yes, I said, that was my father.

Not just my father, now, but the body. The victim.

The funeral rolled around within a week. I was instructed to wear a suit and tie. The only black suit I had was one Dad had bought me for my 21st birthday present.

As I slipped into the jacket, a memory shot through my head. I was running to meet Dad on a rainy evening as he waited for me in the men's section of Harvey Nichols in Knightsbridge, to buy my first suit. Now I was wearing it to bury him.

It was a short ceremony. We didn't have a full service inside, just a small gathering near the grave outside an old Surrey church. The plot stood on its own off to one side of the graveyard, and almost nobody else was around. Only a handful of people came. Mum wasn't allowed to be there.

She had been upset that she wouldn't be let out. But even her distress seemed somehow muffled – as though she was too disorientated to comprehend what was really happening and why.

It rained all day. A vicar who didn't know him reduced Dad's life to a few bullet points. The words washed over me as the coffin was lowered into the ground. We were instructed to throw a handful of earth onto it. I didn't want to. But I had the urge to throw something at someone, and there was dirt in my hand, so I did what I was told.

We gathered at a nearby pub. There was a Coke in front of me on the sticky table, and people were talking around me. They would come up and say a few words, but nothing you could describe as a conversation. Just a smattering of condolences cobbled together.

'He was a good man,' someone said.

'Okay . . . thank you,' I answered.

There didn't seem to be anything else I could add.

Chapter Two

As soon as the news coverage broke, the barrage was ceaseless.

Wife 'kills her womanising husband with a hammer' before driving to Beachy Head and threatening to jump – the *Daily Mail* screamed.

Our neighbours had spoken to the press. One neighbour stated that my parents' split was 'because he [Dad] kept having affairs and seeing prostitutes'. The reporter had obtained various photos of my parents from some unknown online account. The effect was clear to me: it rammed home a black-and-white narrative of killer and victim, devoid of any real human feeling towards us all.

A glance at the Challens' profiles on the Friends Reunited website reveals a snapshot of their troubled marriage.

Richard Challen used his page to make clear his dissatisfaction with his relationship. Describing himself, the businessman wrote: 'Married two children (unfortunately) living in Claygate Esher Surrey.

Another paper showed him standing next to his Ferrari in Italy. This photo was framed in Ruxley Ridge. The reporting felt sensationalised in every detail, seemingly more fixated on the value of my father's assets than the impact on our family.

Then our driveway was on *London Tonight*. Our house, its

red bricks, the white windows, the neat symmetrical bays. A white-overalled forensics officer making his way across the screen. Across the crime scene. The reporter repeating our parents' names. And in the hands of one of the forensics officers: the hammer. The worn wooden handle, the black metal head. I knew that hammer. It was part of the furniture of our lives. It had always sat inconspicuously with the other tools in the passage by the back door at Ruxley Ridge.

I had walked by it over twenty times a day for decades. And now it had become the murder weapon.

We learned this from the news.

I clenched my eyes shut against the knowledge of what that meant, against the shocking reality of what that hammer had inflicted.

After the police released the house at Ruxley Ridge, James, Jen and I had to go back there to collect some things. I told myself it was a matter of steps, one at a time . . .

Drive down the driveway. Open the front door to your childhood home. Walk through the hallway. Do not think of the smell of your father. Do not think of his voice calling from another room. Don't let yourself be overcome by what happened down the corridor. Get what you need to get and leave.

But once I walked through the door, all clarity dissolved. There was a taut, almost feverish atmosphere in the house. All three of us were drawn inexorably to the kitchen. To the scene of it all.

I braced myself for the overpowering smell of disinfectant. I imagined that every surface would have been scrubbed and steamed; all the evidence measured, recorded and then eliminated.

Until I entered the kitchen and realised how wrong I had been. I took in the room. It was as it always had been: a TV hanging on the grey wall, the big window overlooking Mum's beloved garden.

And then my eyes focused properly, and I could see everything else. An arc of drops already turned brown wheeled across the room. On the table. On the floor. Congealed on the heating vents.

My gaze flicked back to the Mercury cooker unit, still laden with the pots and pans Mum had cleaned after cooking his final meal.

My dad's blood: his life, scattered into thousands upon thousands of tiny flecks across the room.

Chapter Three

The windows gave it away. If it wasn't for those, we could have been in any bland public space – a hospital, a public gym, a school.

Sharp echoes bounced off the high ceilings as the blue carpet was quiet under our feet. Amateur art, cheerful plants and colourful chairs softened the starkness of the concrete walls. There was even a kids' area.

But from our seat, next to the floor-to-ceiling windows which ran full span of the room, the bars were the dominant feature. Sturdy white bars reinforcing the glass, top to bottom. The metalwork was emphatic: this was prison. Her Majesty's Prison Bronzefield, in Ashford. A big category-A women's prison, the largest in the country, typically used for women on remand, before those convicted are sentenced to do their time elsewhere.

The brightly coloured chairs weren't a jaunty design choice: they indicated the designated seating areas. Green for the visitors, burgundy for the prisoners. The kids' area looked cheerful until you realised that the children playing in it only ever saw their mothers under these sickly pendant lights. The staff sat behind the big console-like desk in the middle of it all, keeping an eye out for any hugs that lingered too long. The prison guards patrolled the halls, there to observe and control.

It was our first visit.

Since the day my father's body was discovered, the only contact any of us had had with Mum had been the few phone calls she was allowed to make from prison. Every time we spoke, Mum sounded just as concussed and monotone as she had on that first call, almost as if she were drugged. The telephone line felt like a tightrope we were unable to cross. We had managed to go no further than the routine 'How are you doing?'

None of us could figure out an answer. None of us knew what to ask.

Now, about four weeks later, we were finally able to visit her. Confused images of tall grey stone buildings and towering prison gates loomed in my head as we drove towards the prison, but the reality turned out to be a low, modern building: grey roof, pale brick, bright blue signage. James, Jen, Noel and I could barely speak as we pulled into the car park.

In the reception area, we were met with endless pairs of eyes that seemed trained on us. I looked away to the rest of the room: glass screens everywhere, hiving us visitors off from the staff.

We gave Mum's name, reciting for the first time her prison number: HK9446. That's who she was now. *She's my mum. My kind, soft mum.* But to them, she was HK9446. Letters and numbers on a faceless system.

A while later, a guard called out a group of names. We listened out for *Georgina Challen* – her legal name. A group of people slid off their chairs and shuffled through a metal detector to be patted down by a guard. We watched as they squeezed through the closing doors, leaving them shut in a small glass vestibule. There was a lull before they were spat out into another waiting area and the pattern repeated. Group after group were processed, like prodded cattle.

Then it was our turn.

I had been trying my best not to think about what I would say to Mum. My mind was blankness, every word bled out of its existence. The last time we had been together she had been dropping me off for a day of work.

'Georgina Challen,' announced the guard.

All I could see was her face. Her eyes, her mouth an inverted crescent moon. She was sobbing before she reached us. She was dressed like all the other prisoners, in grey joggers and a crew neck. Her face was gaunt. She didn't have her mouth plates in, so it looked as though some of her teeth were missing. Her usually glamorous, sleek blonde hair was a colourless frizz. She looked hollowed out.

We hugged. We had been told we were only allowed to hug her once, so we hung on as long as we could.

'Sally, do you have everything you need?' said Noel urgently.

But Mum wasn't listening. She was peering intently into our faces. I caught the emotions flitting across her face: mania, grief, pain. A picture of loss.

Was she sorry for what she had done to us? Or sorry for what she had destroyed?

'Sally? Are you listening? We don't have much time. What could we send you?' Noel tried again.

Mum's answers were monosyllabic. She clasped my hands in hers. I let her hold them as an anchorage.

'I need clothes and money to buy things . . .' she replied distractedly, before turning to gaze at James.

James and I were both silent. This was too much. This place. The state she was in. What she had done.

I blurted out, 'Why? Why did you do it? Why?'

I was sobbing so much that I was barely intelligible.

Her voice was emotionless, even resigned to her own answer. It was as though she too had come up blank. 'I'm sorry,' she said. 'I don't know.'

It was like she was just saying the only words that she felt she could say. 'I don't know,' over and over again, sounding more deadened with every repetition.

It was the only time I ever asked her why.

I didn't really want an answer.

I couldn't find words for it, even for myself, but I instinctively knew that what had happened wasn't within her control. For weeks beforehand I had seen her very essence ebbing away until she was no longer herself. Whatever impulse had made her do this terrible thing had disappeared as soon as it was done. There was no explanation she could give. I knew that.

'Five minutes. Start saying your goodbyes.'

Mum lived in a world bounded by rules and orders and regulations now. She was standing and hugging us, then turning and walking away. We stood watching as she queued and disappeared.

For hours afterwards, my mind twisted and turned, struggling against the truth.

She was beyond our reach.

Chapter Four

I was adrift.

Throughout my life, my mother had always been my shepherd, my moral touchpoint. I went to her whenever I needed help, and it always came flowing back. But now? She was unreachable. Worse than that. Something in her was broken, perhaps irrevocably.

The threads of my own life were ragged. Not knowing what else to do, I went as planned to university, joining Ian in the flat he had found.

I discovered as soon as I got there that I had made a mistake about the course I was on, and would need to go and see the course director to explain. The idea filled me with dread. It was the first time I would have to tell a stranger what had happened. I sent her an email in advance, unable to find the words. In the end I carefully used the wording from a solicitor's letter to explain what had happened.

Knocking on the course leader's office door, I steeled myself. She was on the phone as I walked in, hanging up with a cheerful smile. 'Hang on,' she said, 'David . . . oh yes, you sent me an email, didn't you? I haven't had a chance to read it yet. Let me just . . .'

The room lurched. I couldn't stand to look at her face as she called my email up on her screen.

'Oh my God, oh my God,' she repeated to herself, her

mouth gaping in horror. The tears came over me like a wave. Suddenly I could see the story through a stranger's eyes. 'David, I'm so sorry. You poor thing.' She reached across her desk, handing me tissues. 'If there's anything I can do . . . please let me know. What do you need?'

I got the permission to move to her course, but joining directly into the second year turned out not to be the best plan. Friendships were already established, groups and cliques full. And I was in no state to try and make myself sociable. I couldn't tell anyone the truth about my life.

My two saviours were Ian and my partner Anthony, who came and stayed with me as much as he could. He'd find me staring out of the window of the flat, watching the waves of the sea violently crashing into one another.

To survive, I started to learn a skill I would come to perfect in the coming years: how to detach and compartmentalise. For five days of the week, I would not think about Mum, and walk myself through the appearance of a normal student existence. Then, every weekend, I would clock into a different life, and would travel to HMP Bronzefield to see her.

That year, I spent Christmas with Jen. Her family were doing their best, but visions of past Christmases – Mum handing out pigs in blankets and cheese wrapped in bacon round our tree – haunted me. As did the present-day version of mum, spectral in her grey sweatshirt, locked in a prison cell.

We had managed to get a visiting slot as close to Christmas day as possible, but it was hard to feel any festive cheer. The prison had made an effort to decorate the visitor areas. Strands of tinsel and Christmas tree cut-outs adorned the walls. Some of the more cheerful guards were sporting floppy Santa hats. But all I could see were the countless Christmases awaiting us, just like this one.

And then I saw Mum's hopeful face coming towards us. We did our best to perk up, but everything felt stilted.

'I've bought you presents,' she said. 'You can pick them up as you leave. They'll hand them to you.'

We nodded numbly. And before we could find a rhythm, the five-minute warning came. We tacked a hollow 'Happy Christmas, Mum' to the end of our goodbye hugs before heading for the exit. Mum sat marooned at her table, waiting for her name to be called as she watched us walk away.

A prison guard on the far side of the turnstile handed me something. A cellophane-wrapped wicker basket, filled with small treats: chocolate bars, miscellaneous sweets, a cuddly stuffed toy. There was row after row of baskets, shiny and crackling in their garish wrapping.

'It's from your mum. The prisoners are allowed to buy these Christmas packages for their family members,' the guard explained.

I looked back her, her hopeful facing beaming at me. The stuffed teddy bear stared unblinkingly up at me through plastic film. I felt like a small child.

It destroyed me.

All around us were families standing up from their own visits, gathering their things. The awfulness of it all hit me.

And I knew we were at least far enough down the line to have some perspective. We had had our childhood Christmases already. But those other families, the small children who would treasure those little stuffed animals: some of them were too young even to understand why their mothers weren't going to be with them on Christmas day.

James and I didn't speak until we got home, the two Christmas baskets rustling in the back seat as we parked up.

Chapter Five

In the days following the arrest, Mum's brothers had quickly rallied to her cause. Terence and Nigel, as well as my cousin Hugo, were having endless conversations, just out of earshot, about how to get the best possible legal representation.

They would move as a group into another room to have these discussions, putting a physical barrier between us and them. It felt as though I was being treated as 'one of the children'. I wanted to be involved. I had been kept out of the loop before, and that lack of awareness had cost me everything.

But it was hard to break the force field of authority that surrounded them. They lived in a world of boardrooms and big decisions, peopled by men with suits and smooth rhetoric. They knew how to get things done.

I knew I needed to do something, but I couldn't find an entry point, so I spoke to Anthony in desperation. His friend's father was a well-known criminal barrister. He arranged a call. I crept upstairs out of everyone's way, telling him the full story in a hushed voice on my knees.

'Right, okay . . . Do you know what she has been charged with?'

'I . . . I don't know,' I said, floundering for answers.

He talked me through the basics. What it meant if Mum was charged and went on remand – that she would be in prison until she came to trial. How long the process of getting to trial would take. It all sounded bleak – because it was bleak.

All of this meant that Ruxley Ridge had to be sold. I was told that we had to go in and choose what we wanted to keep. We had one last chance to dash through the rooms of our childhood home, as though the house was on fire and there were only moments to decide what to save.

We had also agreed to a mad plan that Mum had come up with, to store some of the furniture in a barn belonging to the brother of a fellow prisoner – which is how we ended up loading her carefully chosen furniture into a grubby horse trailer. Her beautiful cream sofa, the black lacquered sideboards, chests of drawers and the dressing table I had loved as a child: all jumbled up and piled inside the trailer.

We followed the trailer as it bumped along country roads to a strange barn in some desolate fields. A small Jack Russell terrier yapped and ran around our feet as we unloaded the contents. The cream-coloured sofa sat stranded amid the dirt, paw prints marking the covers.

Then we went back to Ruxley Ridge for the final time. Patches on the walls betrayed where the pictures used to hang. I darted into empty rooms where I needed nothing, just to take one last mental snapshot. The door to the kitchen remained closed. I didn't want to go in there again. But the horror that seeped from behind its doors stained the whole house.

The new owners said we had left a plasma TV hanging on one of the walls. The one my dad had guarded so closely.

Once that was dealt with, my childhood home was gone.

Chapter Six

The exterior of the building was brutalist. Its interiors were plush and kitted out with sound-deadening carpets. Our lead solicitor, Jonathan Grimes, appeared to be quite young – in his thirties – but somehow imposing. He reflected the air of confidence that seemed to emanate from the building itself. I convinced myself that this was reassuring: our solicitor wasn't troubled by our predicament – this was just another job for him. We were in good hands. My uncles, James and I gathered round a large mahogany table in a boardroom. They had selected these lawyers to represent Mum.

The basic fact that she had killed my father was not in dispute. The case would instead hinge on her state of mind at the time of the killing. The best result we could hope for, he told us, would be manslaughter with diminished responsibility. She would be looking at a sentence of about eight years, probably coming out on parole in about four or five. The worst case was murder. This would carry a life sentence. But the judge was likely to set a minimum term before she could apply for release on parole. That minimum term would be at least 15 years.

I sat at that mahogany table, trying my best to understand what these unfamiliar terms meant. He told us that my brother and I were going to be called as witnesses for the prosecution, which I had not expected. What I had expected was that our defence team would ask James and me to take to the stand to bear witness to our father's dominance over our mother – to tell truths that would sketch in the enormous blank space at the core of what had happened.

But any points we raised about Dad's behaviour towards Mum weren't part of the case, on the basis that it always plays badly with juries to speak ill of the dead. Only the bare facts – the brothel visit, the police call, the arguments – were mentioned. They didn't delve any further beyond this point.

A psychiatrist had been called in to assess Mum. He had come back with a diagnosis of depression, which was going to form the heart of the 'diminished responsibility' plea.

But to me, the vague diagnosis of 'depression' didn't touch the sides of our reality, the reality we had faced every day for 23 years. To me it was clear that Dad's nature and behaviour throughout their marriage and my childhood was a huge factor – the only possible way of making sense of it. If we weren't going to be talking about that, then the whole trial seemed senseless. The whole shape of their marriage, the whole shape of their lives, had been controlled by Dad. But I couldn't find the right words to describe things as they really had been. To explain the dominance and destruction that took place before my mother ever picked up that hammer.

Instead, they walked us through how the court case would work: how we would be called to give evidence. How up to that point we would not be able to watch proceedings, but that afterwards we could join the public gallery, and what would happen when we took the stand.

A couple of weeks later the solicitors introduced us to the barrister that they had instructed, Patrick Gibbs QC. He was a towering, bespectacled man with a slender frame and the same sheen of authority about him as Jonathan Grimes. Everything about him was confidence and measured poise.

The trial date was set shortly thereafter: 14 June 2011. That date began to overshadow everything in our lives. It ground towards us with the force of a sixteen-wheeler, inexorably coming ever closer. And just as it was nearly on top of us, a significant revelation came to light.

It concerned the hammer.

It changed everything.

Chapter Seven

I hadn't wanted to picture the sequence of events that led
to the unthinkable, but I had drawn it out somewhere in
my mind: Mum had gone over to Ruxley Ridge. Dad had,
somehow, pushed her too far. And, driven outside of herself,
she had picked up the first thing that came to hand: the
hammer that had always sat in the little passage beyond the
kitchen. It made sense to me, given how she had been in
the weeks before. The detachment, the haziness, and then a
moment of pure madness. That's the only way I could make
sense of it.

James and I settled down in the navy-blue prison chairs, and
Mum shifted to look at us more closely. She seemed especially
apprehensive that day, her hands visibly shaking in front
of her.

'I have something I need to tell you both,' she began.

Her head began to bow, but she maintained eye contact.

'I brought the hammer with me from Ashton.'

Are you serious? I thought.

In that godforsaken moment, it dawned on me that
the hammer, which I had always known to live next to the
kitchen at home, had in fact come with us to Ashton Place.
I had never noticed it, but during the year of their separation,
it had actually been in our possession, not Dad's. So at some

point, Mum had placed the hammer in her handbag, carried her handbag through the front door at Ruxley and into the kitchen where she set about preparing my Dad's lunch.

What could she possibly have been thinking?

In her original statement to the police, after they had talked her down from Beachy Head and taken her into custody, Mum had stated that she'd grabbed the hammer at Ruxley Road. The next day, she had spoken to them again and corrected that statement.

Everything I thought I knew, for the best part of a year, about how and why she had come to commit this act, fell away.

This was my first moment of doubt.

I didn't know what to say. She was terrified. I couldn't press her on the details in that moment. Even if I could have, I knew she wasn't in any state to shed light on it.

We sat on the now-familiar chairs with as much clarity as on our first visit. The minutes passed in a haze of tears – we were all still so lost.

But I knew I couldn't bury this information inside myself and just move on. It would be as if I was burying something nuclear. I'd be poisoning my soul. I knew I had to freeze what I felt, and try to confront myself. I had to question myself, be absolutely sure. And that meant removing as much emotion as I could from my assumptions.

Back in Brighton, I spent days and hours turning it over in my head. The seafront beckoned me, the waves swirling to titanic sizes.

I was pushing hard up against everything I knew about my mother now, questioning whether I had been right to stand by her. I had to think, really think about what I believed. It had never occurred to me that a 'moment of madness' could be anything more than a moment. That it could expand and stretch and eat away hours, if not days, or possibly weeks.

However I looked at it, I felt certain that what she had done wasn't calculated. It wasn't an act of malice. Because I knew that she just didn't have that within her.

I looked at the situation from all angles.

I thought carefully about how Mum had been in the days leading up to Dad's death, about her momentary lapses of attention in those days and weeks before.

I had spoken to her in the kitchen, watching as she washed up, her body moving through the motions, her mind elsewhere.

I had heard her voice, and its strange quality on the phone when I realised she was at Ruxley: tangled up, emotional, caught between two places.

I had felt the spaces in the home where she should have been, but was not.

I had not realised what was happening within her. How something inside her was running away from itself.

I had always thought of losing control as an instantaneous thing, a snapping, but maybe I had been wrong? Maybe it was not always loud or sudden. Maybe sometimes it was quieter, like a structure weakening from the inside. I pictured cliffs along the coast, how they stand up tall and immovable, how they seem solid right up until the moment they collapse. But the fall is never just the fall. It starts long before that: years of waves pulling at the foundations, salt and wind eating away at them bit by bit. The collapse is just the final part, the moment everything gives way. Not a break, not a single moment, but an erosion.

It dawned on me then that it had been happening in front of my eyes, and I had ignored it. I had been there. I had seen her. I had known something was wrong, yet I had done nothing. Just as Noel had tried and then closed the door to her, discouraging her from speaking about Dad any more. All of us had, somewhere along the line, shut down that conversation.

She was left alone with her thoughts, until she had fewer and fewer avenues of escape, until the only way to save herself was to go back to him.

But it was not a way out; it was a trap back to the life she'd had before. Nothing had changed. Her sense of self was lost.

All of Mum's actions led back to the original starting point: she had been driven outside herself. She hadn't been in her right mind. And whether that period lasted for a moment or hours, it eventually amounted to the same thing. It didn't change what I had first known to be true – that my mother had killed my father – but the roots of this act lay in the years preceding it. The wheels had been put in motion long ago.

Where the hammer had come from didn't change that.

Chapter Eight

Guildford Crown Court was a single-storey, red-brick modern building, its strange pointed tower adorned with the royal coat of arms stamping it with the authority of the state.

We huddled together outside the building, everything before us a great, terrible unknown.

'I don't understand what we're meant to say on the stand,' Jen said, visibly panicked.

'Just tell the truth,' Noel said repeatedly. 'The truth will set you free.'

We were ushered into a waiting room where we would while away the hours while our mother's court case began. As James, Jen, Noel and I were going to be called as witnesses, we weren't allowed to watch the trial until we had given our testimony. From time to time, we picked at the snacks provided. The FLOs would occasionally poke their heads in to check on us. It was unbearable, to know that Mum was somewhere in this same building, and that we weren't able to see her or support her. A trial about our family, one that would affect every day of the rest of our lives, was playing out to a room full of strangers.

The lawyers would have made their opening statements by now. How far in were they? What were they talking about? What did the jury think? Was it going well? Was it going badly? During the break, I met my partner Anthony in the canteen. He was watching from the public gallery. He looked visibly traumatised from listening to the opening remarks. How could I possibly have warned him?

Noel went first, and then, in the afternoon, the FLO came in and called my name. She walked me to the doors of the courtroom and pushed them open. Taking a deep breath, I went through. It was the first time I had laid eyes on a courtroom, and now I was to be the centre of its attention.

Ranks of faces in the public gallery turned in my direction as I walked in. I came in through the side door and had to walk across the whole courtroom to reach the witness box. Past the prosecution lawyers and the defence lawyers. Past the rows of benches where the jury was sitting. It was all a white wall of eyes.

When I eventually reached the stand, my legs had begun to shake. And then I saw Mum, sitting at the back. She looked tiny, her face cast down. I had to look away.

'Do you swear to tell the truth, the whole truth, and nothing but the truth?' the court usher demanded.

In the public seats behind me I could make out Anthony and Noel, but it was too much to look at them. I tried to focus elsewhere. The jury sat right in my eyeline, and I fixed on the blankness of their faces. The strangeness of twelve total strangers whose decision would affect the rest of our lives.

The barrister for the prosecution, Caroline Carberry QC, stood up swiftly. Her sharp focus felt hawk-like under her wig, her eyes boring into me.

She opened her questions by noting that I lived with my

mother at the time of the incident, and seemed to be circling around my poor relationship with Dad.

'Would you describe your relationship as good or not?' she fired at me.

She kept up her questions for fifteen minutes. It felt to me that one minute she would shoot questions at me, without giving me time to compose myself, and the next she would turn away from me mid-answer, as though my answer were irrelevant.

'At Ashton Place, did you see much of each other?'

'You were working long shifts, working late – did you feel as close to her as you once did?'

'Did she tell you her plans for the future?'

Then she was peppering me with questions about the night before Mum's arrest.

My hands on the rail shook.

She eventually ceded to the defence barrister. Patrick Gibbs was slower; he took his time. Everything about his oratorial style seemed designed to deliver a sense of deep calm. His hands floated up to meet in front him as he paused to think.

He asked about our family dynamics, moving quickly over the brothel incident and my father's dominant nature. I began to fear I wouldn't get the chance to tell this court the truth. Our full truth.

I looked at him beseechingly. I wanted to be allowed to expand.

'Mum wasn't the happy person she once was. She was controlled by my father,' I blurted out.

I tried to paint a picture of the rabbit hole of madness that Dad had sent Mum down. The ways he made her question reality, how he had pushed her into thinking she was insane. I saw a juror's face break into what I thought was sympathy, and that was it. I started sobbing. The judge asked me to take a moment. A fresh glass of water was passed to me by the clerk. I took a sip, wiping away my tears with tissues from a box that appeared next to me.

More questions. And then it was over.

'You may leave the stand,' the judge said.

I was to take my place in the public gallery, but I needed to get out. I walked through the court as fast as I could go, burst out of the final set of doors into the empty foyer and ground to a halt. There was nowhere left for me to go.

Sarah, the FLO, had been watching the proceedings and caught up with me, putting her arm around me.

'David, it's okay, are you okay? Do you want to sit down? What do you want to do?'

I could barely speak, my cheeks slack with my cold tears.

'You don't have to go back in, you know. Not unless you want to,' Sarah said.

'No,' I said, 'I have to go back. My whole world, whole family is inside that room.'

And so the days ground on, witness after witness. Neighbours, colleagues, friends describing phone calls they'd had with my mother, the concerns they had for her state of mind, how she was manic one day and sullen the next.

'Richard was her world, and she focused on him,' said her close friend, Sarah Noble. She even used the word bipolar to describe Mum, and talked about how controlling the proposed postnuptial agreement was.

They read statements from random people Dad had met on singles holidays and dating websites. Some guy who he had shared a taxi with in Vietnam described him as 'a pleasant, gentle chap'. Another lady, that he'd presumably been on a date with, had called him 'a gentleman'.

These testimonies seemed to be afforded equal weight with ours. The picture the prosecution was painting soon crystallised: a long-suffering man trying to put himself back together in the wake of a painful divorce from a jealous woman.

Some people, like me, used the word controlling about Dad. But it seemed to have no traction. It was as though that was just part of the normal dynamics of marriage. I could see my brother on the other side of the aisle, the nape of his neck tensed up in anger.

The worst came when the prosecution produced a recording to share with the court. I knew exactly what it was the minute it began playing. It was like being stripped naked – one of the lowest moments of our lives, blasted out into the courtroom.

It was the call Mum had made to the police on the night that the news covered the brothel raid. I thought back to that night, sitting on the landing, listening to Mum's pleas of desperation. Her voice rang out through the courtroom in all its anger. I knew exactly what was coming:

'And is Mr Challen there?' asked the operator.

'No,' said Mum, her voice completely flat. 'He's dead.'

In the dead silence of the courtroom, I closed my eyes in despair.

Then Dad came on the line. The shock of hearing his voice again, the voice we had buried only months before, managing to reach out from beyond the grave and impose his narrative even in death.

The operator's voice was sympathetic as she responded to my Dad's quavering 'Hello . . .' To her, this was a downtrodden husband dealing with a drunken wife.

But James and I looked at each another, shaking our heads knowingly. We knew that voice. It was the 'play-acting' voice. The wheedling voice he'd used all those times he had hidden in the playroom with us.

'Do you need assistance?' the call handler asked compassionately.

Again, the fake tremor as he explained that his wife was drunk. The fake hesitation when the call handler asked if there had been any violence. 'No . . .' he said slowly. 'No . . .'

I wanted to scream at the whole court. But our testimonies were over. The Richard Challen the court had been shown was a successful, charming businessman who provided for his family and gave them everything, and even put up with the waywardness of his difficult wife. I caught sight of one of the jurors. His face appeared to be overcome with sympathy.

At some point later on, a DVD player was wheeled into the courtroom and it played the recording of Mum's police interview. She sat in a navy sweatshirt, flanked by her lawyer and two police officers taking notes. Her face looked drawn, as if she hadn't slept for a week, her hair a mess. Her eyes were cast down, dead when they looked up. She was talking very slowly, her pauses stretching out interminably. I couldn't take in what she was saying, as I was transfixed by what must have been going through her mind at that moment.

At lunchtimes, we all gathered in the small cafeteria. It was hard to talk, with police, witnesses and lawyers all crammed into tiny tables. We tried to keep our heads down.

'What hope do we have if we can't say anything negative about him?' Terence railed, pacing back and forth. 'It's utterly ridiculous.'

'We have to trust the system and just allow the court to hear the case,' Noel finally said.

The truth shall set you free? How could the truth set you free when the truth wasn't allowed out? And then it was Mum's turn to come on the stand. Nothing could have prepared me for how torturous it would be to witness her testimony. She was a zombie. She wasn't there. No matter what accusation was hurled at her, she could only reply: 'I suppose so,' again and again. 'I suppose I did.' 'I must have.' Or simply, 'Yes.'

It didn't seem to occur to her to try and defend her case. She agreed with everything that was put to her. Question after question rained down about the hammer – when did she bring it? Why did she bring it? Why didn't she tell the police about it immediately?

To all of it, she could only say she didn't recall, she didn't know, she couldn't believe she had done it. There was a blank acceptance of the horror of it all.

She was asked about seeing a doctor for her state of mind. She had gone a few times in 2007, again in 2008, then six times in 2009. Stress, mostly. And then, nothing. After

October 2009, it was like she disappeared from their records. She had been prescribed medication, but never took it.

'Why hadn't you gone back in 2010?' she was asked.

She didn't have an answer.

She described how she wasn't getting up at the weekend. How she was only getting up to take me to work and going back to bed afterwards. The word she used was 'flat'.

'I didn't feel like myself. I don't know what "myself" was.'

The cruellest blows came when Carberry brought up the suicide note Mum had left in the kitchen, noting that she had written suicide notes before this.

'If you wanted to kill yourself, why is it that when you realised the dreadful damage you had done, you didn't go ahead?'

'I don't know, I didn't think,' whispered Mum.

I didn't know that she'd been writing suicide notes all along.

'You knew how to from your history of research on how to slit your wrists,' said Caroline Carberry. 'Why not take a knife from the kitchen and do it?'

I clung to the court bench, desperate to remain strong, but tears streamed down my face.

Dr Exworthy, the psychiatrist for the defence, was up next. He argued that Mum had a pattern of depression dating back to 2004, that she had been in the grip of a depressive episode at the time of the incident. He evidenced this claim with previous doctor's visits over the past five years, the way people had noticed her low mood and lack of energy in the days prior to the killing, and her 'poor self-care'.

Dr Gilluley, the psychiatrist for the Crown Prosecution Service who had interviewed Mum after her arrest, came up to argue against this claim. He asserted that Mum was not suffering from depression or any mental difficulty when she killed Dad. He focused on her ability to function and paid less attention to her suicidal ideation and obvious unhappiness she had radiated to friends and colleagues. According to him, this could be explained away by the fact she was in an unhappy marriage and was drinking too much.

Jen was the last witness. She did her best, describing how Mum had confided in her about how Dad would belittle her, and how broken Mum's confidence was. When she came down, her face was pained, like the rest of us.

In her summing up, Caroline Carberry seemed to focus on her argument that Mum couldn't have been depressed because she put make-up on in the mornings.

I could see only one way this would go. I watched the jury closely throughout the judge's lengthy final speech. Many of the jury members seemed to me to share a pained expression, even the ones who I felt had succeeded in carefully keeping emotion from their faces until this point.

They spent a day in discussions. As they filed back in on the second day, I knew what their verdict was. In fact, I had known already, even as they left the courtroom. The route towards their decision was so narrow and limited: there was just no other way out for them. If anything, I felt pity for them, for what they were about to do to us.

I had lived in this family, inside that home. I knew the control Dad wielded, the way reality was bent to fit his version of events. But I also knew, long before the verdict was even spoken, that none of it had come across.

The court had stripped everything down to what could

be proven, what fit inside the legal arguments available. Her life, and ours, were reduced to a fragment of time. The jury were bound, like us, by the limits of what they were allowed to see and hear.

A court official's voice rang out:

'Mr Foreman, please answer my next question either yes or no. Has the jury reached verdicts on which you are all agreed?'

'Yes.'

'And on this indictment of murder, do you find Georgina Challen guilty or not guilty?'

'Guilty.'

A silence swept the courtroom as the judge and clerks noted down the outcome. Then, I heard it. James's tears. It was all I could hear. It was all anyone could hear. It sounded like his soul was being ripped out of his body right in front of us. I had never heard a noise like it before. It echoed and filled the room.

I felt white, blank. It was as though the blow had landed somewhere very far away. I looked for it, waiting for the pain to hit.

I finally forced myself to look at my mother. Her head was down, her face completely closed. She wiped away a single tear.

The judge was still speaking. He sentenced her right then and there. A life sentence. A minimum term of eighteen years.

The judge then left the courtroom briefly before returning to say one last thing. There was something he hadn't factored into the sentencing: the aggravating factor of bringing a weapon to the scene of the crime. For that, he was adding another four years, bringing the minimum term up to twenty-two years.

Twenty-two years.

It was almost the length of my entire life.

AWAKENING

Chapter One

The world had decided who it thought my mum was. The media painted her as a vengeful woman who 'counted his Viagra pills' and 'spied' on her husband. A woman led to murder by 'jealousy'.

I knew, we knew, who she really was. A woman grappling with reality itself. Trying to find the truth that my father had buried.

The days after the court case had been a blur of greyness. There was nothing. I wasn't crying, or shouting, or going over and over things. I went upstairs, and lay on top of my bed, staring at the ceiling.

Jen popped her head round the door at one point to ask if there was anything I needed.

'Have you cried yet?' she asked, worried about me.

'No,' I said. I was locked inside my body.

Some days later, I walked into the living room at Ashton Place to find some boxes that the solicitors had sent over. Big encyclopaedic folders which contained all the statements from all the police witnesses. It had arrived some days ago and had been sitting in the living room like a black hole, drawing everything around it into its forcefield. I wasn't sure I could cope with opening it, revisiting all the evidence, hearing all about the psychiatrist's assessments, ploughing through the arguments and counter arguments about Mum's depression once again, rereading the brutal, cold, note-like details of our lives.

But something in me burnt white hot with need. I wanted to know it all. Everything I hadn't been told. Or had been told only half of. I needed to see for myself now – and it was all inside these boxes.

As soon as I opened the files, I knew they would take over every inch of my mind. Sheaf after sheaf of paper, with its double-spaced type. Statements taken from friends and family, colleagues and acquaintances.

Here was my brother detailing how Mum tried to lose weight because of Dad's comments: 'You could do with losing a bit more'.

Here he was describing how Dad didn't like Mum speaking to Jen because she became more confident when she had friends.

Here was Jen, explaining how my father would turn questions about his infidelities around on my mother and blame her for being paranoid, even crazy.

Here was me, describing how Dad would repeatedly tell her 'you're insane'. How she would then ask James and me if she was imagining things, and questioned herself about whether she was going mad, over and over.

Here was her boss, talking about a time he had found her in tears after Dad had called her fat and made her change her clothes before an evening out. How my father discouraged her from going to work conferences.

Here was one of Mum's colleagues, someone I didn't know, telling the police about Dad's prostitutes and the salsa dancing, how he called my mum fat and ugly. And then how my mother had changed in the last years, becoming a shadow of herself.

Here was Sarah Noble, describing Dad as a controlling person.

Here was Mum's old friend Debbie Giles: 'To my mind, Richard was like a drug to Sally. She knew he was not good for her but she couldn't live without him.'

And her colleague, who had known her for over a decade: 'I had never seen Sally angry. She is more likely to run the other way than confront anyone due to her lack of confidence and self-worth. I find this incident deeply upsetting and unbelievable.'

And then there was Mum: pages and pages of statements from her, typed up and logged into some police databases. An outpouring. There was no order to it all – she had used the police interviews as a kind of confessional, the secrets of her whole marriage spilt out of her unchecked. Her story looped around, going off on tangents, her thoughts pouring forth as they occurred to her. There was no artifice, no pretence.

Here was the real history, as if all this time I had been watching silhouettes and shadows, and suddenly here were my parents in 3D technicolour.

I tried to start at their beginning. The story I had known of two young lovers, meeting early, their love overcoming the opposition of her family, until they finally came together in those sunlit English wedding photographs. Faded to black. Mum had been only fifteen to Dad's twenty-one when they met. A child. Her whole life ahead of her. A child who, six years later, took an overdose after a row about another woman he had started seeing at the same time as her.

Everything was on Richard's terms, she told the police, a note of acceptance coming off the page.

We got married. We had children only when he was ready. And once, when I thought that I was pregnant, he said, 'Well, we're not having any more so if you are you'll have to have an abortion', she said, adding that she put up with his controlling side because she loved him.

I read how her role, as defined by him, was to be *wholly responsible for bringing up the children, to help build up his business and have supper ready on time, on the table every night.* How she had to do all the washing and the ironing and the cooking and the shopping, plus look after her elderly mother and her in-laws. If there was an argument, *I was always the one sort of saying sorry. And I never understood why I was always saying sorry.*

There was still more: secrets hidden from my view as a child. Here was her suspicion that he had been unfaithful to her when I was a baby. How he had forced her to give up work. And how she'd have to constantly go to my father for money to look after James and me. How he'd always make her ask, not offer. How he blamed her for my being gay because her brother was too. She had concealed all of this from us, out of motherly love.

Next I reached the statement from Dr Gilluley, the psychiatrist retained by the CPS, who mentioned the LA holiday, back when I was 11. The holiday that had changed the foundation blocks of our family.

I slowed myself down, here trying to recall my own memories. Yes – here were the familiar details. Del's house. My birthday. The quick kiss. The argument. These things I knew to be true.

Then everything went very still for a moment. I could hear the blood beat in my veins as I read: *She told me that he forced her to have anal sex against her consent.*

I read the passage back. Once, twice, three times. All to be sure. The nausea rose inside of me. Surely this couldn't be right? Surely this was something we should know about? Perhaps Mum's lawyers somehow didn't know?

I flicked to the statement from the other psychiatrist, the one retained by the defence:

Here it was, the same story. And then: *She told me that later that evening Mr Challen forced her onto the bed and 'raped me from behind' (by which she meant buggery) as 'a punishment'.*

I was catapulted back to the morning after my birthday in LA, to those long silent moments in the car as we'd driven away from Del's house under grey skies all those years before. Dad's tightly suppressed fury, Mum muted and cowed beside him. Suddenly, it all made mangled and twisted sense. The night before, my father had raped my mother. To punish her.

I flicked back to something that I saw her friend Debbie Giles had said in her statement. How Mum had told her that, after that holiday, Dad had punished her further by confiscating her gold necklace. Revulsion forced its way into my throat.

I sat still for a moment with the file open across my legs, paralysed by what I was reading. I was in my Mum's house, on my own, when it was far, far too late, and there it was, right in front of me. This terrible, monstrous truth. The unthinkable.

It was as though I was trapped in a nightmare, one where

your legs can't move and the panic rises as you realise you can't save yourself. Or anyone around you.

Here I was, rummaging around a box discovering the real story of my life. Both the Crown and defence psychiatrists had this information in their reports, but it wasn't presented at trial. Not only that, but they had even said there was no violence in the marriage. No violence? When this was in their own report? Did rape not count as violence?

We had sat through the whole of that long, drawn-out criminal trial, and endured endless discussions about whether or not my mother had depression. And at no point had anybody mentioned that she was anally raped while married to my father, as a punishment.

Here was the truth of my family. Of my life. Of all the things that I couldn't put together. That unsettling feeling I'd had about Dad as a child. Here was the full picture, stuffed into a file, shuffled into papers, and buried in a box. It was too late.

A dull, throbbing anger settled over me, a bitterness that began to beat in my veins and didn't let up. Not that day, or the next, or in the months and years to come.

I felt I was the one buried six feet under with these terrible truths.

Chapter Two

In prison, Mum's life fell into a shapeless, lifeless state. She existed in purgatory filled only with memories of the past.

I tried to raise what I had read in the lawyers' files with her. 'Mum,' I said, 'I read your statements . . . and the psychiatrists' reports.' But she remained monosyllabic. She had once submitted to the life my father had given her; now she submitted to life in prison. More than anything, she missed Dad. She still loved him, she said, caressing the wedding ring still on her finger. He had been her soulmate, and now she had to learn to live without him.

All the unhappiness he had caused her was part of the deal. The pitch of rage, or anguish, or confusion, or whatever emotion she had reached that had caused her to kill him had passed. Once she had acted on it, that part of her brain was closed off from her forever.

Collectively, we would sit in an almost silent vacuum amid the convivial noise of other visits going on behind us. Jen did her best to keep things upbeat and light.

'Right, Sally, what say we get you some snacks? You always say the food is terrible.'

Mum was never a big eater, but by now she had become paper thin and had aged what seemed like a decade.

I found myself volunteering to go with Jen to get snacks, avoiding the emotional chasm of sitting alone with Mum.

Her deer-like eyes would peer up at me as though I had some answers for her, but I was as lost as she was.

On the train back, I would often find myself thinking back to that first night after the disaster, when Dad appeared to me at the end of my bed, unable to move or communicate with me. Although my mum was still alive, she had become a living spectre, just as he had been.

Every week we would congregate at Ashton Place before heading off to prison. There would be a measure of grim camaraderie as we gathered in Mum's old kitchen. But soon that would also come to an end. Mum needed to rent it out to pay for her lawyers. This was the second house we had to dismantle and pack up. This time it was Mum's personal belongings: her dresses, her perfumes and – worst – her cooking things.

Into the boxes went Granny Jenney's special knife, Mum's beloved pots and pans. It was hard not to think about how long it would be before she might use them again. So instead, I took them and cooked with them as much as I could. They became totems in my life, mementos of happier times. When her cooking timer broke one day, a tear ran down my cheek.

And the truth is, my life quickly became as shapeless as hers. I felt marked, different from anyone else, more like a loner than ever. I was in my final year at Brighton, immersed in my dissertation. I peeled myself away from the trauma of the court only to hide away in a shadowy corner of the university library.

Everything in my life had become a haze. I felt like an alien walking among the students on my course. Making friends was a ship that I had long let sail. My mother was in prison and I was free, but it was as though part of me was locked up in there with Mum. The shadow of her existence never left me.

I would be in my forties when she could first be released, and she in her late seventies. On the train one day, I noticed a guy my age sitting with his mother. They were clearly having a day out. A good lunch, a walk around the shops, perhaps a movie. For them, it was probably a routine day they might not remember in a month's time. For me, it was a vision of the impossible. My partner Anthony was still in my life, juggling his time between his home in Windsor and seeing me in Brighton. When I sank to depths of despair, he'd write me emails championing how far I'd come. When he was overcome with the stress of his work, I'd do the same. But for all the support he offered me, Anthony was powerless to help.

Mum was living for the phone calls from the few members of the family she was calling: James, Jen, me, Mum's niece-in-law Dalla, Noel, her brothers. And we wrote to each other, encouraging ourselves to hang in there.

Dear Mum, I know it can be unimaginable to look forward, at times it is for me too, but please remember to take everything week by week, and even day by day if you need to, develop a routine and stay positive. Write back to me and I will write back to you . . .

Dear David, thank you for your letter. It's very difficult to look forward, but I will try to listen to what you say. It's very bleak, but if you promise to keep moving forward, I will try my best to be there for you too . . .

I had a landline installed in my flat just for her, as calling mobiles from prison was costly. The ring became synonymous with Mum, its loud ring pealing through my head and jerking me back to her reality.

'Hi, it's me, your mother. How are you?' came the voice over the other end of the line. The calls were soundtracked by the shouting of women in the background.

'I'm okay, thanks. Doing a lot of dissertation writing, getting on,' I would reply.

'Okay, well, do the best you can. Are you getting the help you need?'

'Yes, yes. I'm fine. How are you?' I would say, deflecting the attention.

'I'm okay, yes. Tell me, have you been to any nice restaurants?' she asked.

She had started asking me to describe the meals I was eating, relishing every tiny detail. Prison food was all cubes of bland chicken-like substances. If they had chicken drumsticks, it was always the left leg. It seemed a small favour, to indulge her by describing a feast. But sharing my life with her made me feel as though a part of me was ebbing away.

After I left university, I moved into Anthony's family home in Windsor and got a job in a charity call centre. It was arduous, stressful work. My head wasn't in the right place to call people first thing in the morning and ask for money. I had been put on a high dose of medication for depression and all the job made me do was panic.

I became particularly close to Anthony's mother, Susan, or Sue, as she was known to everyone. I felt like I was learning how to be part of a family again, which gave me a sense of togetherness I hadn't realised I desperately needed. But the gratitude was spiked with guilt. I knew Anthony couldn't support me any more, but I didn't have the guts to bring things to a head. The longer I spent with his family, the deeper in I was rooting myself. It wasn't just a relationship I would be saying goodbye to if we split up; it was a home.

I finally found a place to buy: a two-bedroom flat in Cricklewood. Any last-ditch thoughts that Anthony could eventually move in with me were swiftly quashed the first time I took him there.

'What do you think?' I asked walking back to his bus stop home, brimming over with the excitement.

'I don't really like Cricklewood,' he said. We didn't break up then, but it was that moment that sealed our fate.

The morning I left the house in Windsor nearly broke me. I knocked on Sue's bedroom door to say goodbye. It felt like I was throwing myself into the wilderness. But I couldn't tell Mum more than the bare bones of this – I just didn't know how to. I couldn't even bear to print off pictures of my flat to show her. I hated myself for what felt like cruelty, but I could only get through it if I kept a part of myself separate. We had made a pact to survive for each other, and I intended to keep it.

More often than not, Mum also didn't want to talk about what was happening on the inside. For reasons that were never clear to us, she stayed at the remand prison for much longer than expected. Prisoners usually moved on after a short while, but Mum was kept there for six years. During those years, we lived under a perpetual fear that she might suddenly be moved to the other end of the country.

She was quickly put to work. First on laundry, then cleaning, and eventually on the induction system, helping other prisoners on the computers. She had a ringside seat by the revolving door of prison life, seeing the same prisoners return again and again.

A couple of years in, Mum suddenly became manic, calling everyone in the family ten times more often, speaking at speed about everything and anything when we did pick up. She would ask James to source specific clothes for her, or give me strange calls telling me what recipe to cook and film to watch. On visits she would be twitching in her seat, unable to sit still. Her energy was febrile, dizzy-making.

And then after the highs came the enormous lows. She'd disappear into a dark void. All the phone calls would stop. Our letters would remain unopened and unanswered. On visits, her voice sounded weathered.

I too shut myself off. I gave up the job in the call centre. Every dark thought that had once fleetingly passed through my mind now took permanent residence.

My friend Scott and his family looked out for me after I split up with Anthony. One Christmas, he took me to a friend's party. As we pulled up, it hit. The familiar freeze. My chest locked, my hands clung to the car seat.

'I can't do it. I'm sorry . . . I can't,' I stammered.

Scott looked pained, but gentle. 'It's okay. Take a minute. If you feel like coming in, just text. I'll come get you.'

He left me there and I sat ashamed, terrified that I couldn't move. That the darkness was claiming me.

Then his friend's mum came out. I sank lower in my seat, feeling five years old.

'Hi, David. Are you okay? Do you need anything?'

I was mortified. But something about her voice, calm, kind, loosened the knot in my throat.

'I'm just . . . struggling,' I said, searching for words to explain.

She crouched down to my level. 'I'm so sorry. You don't have to come in. But you can, whenever you want. Take your time.'

I nodded, exhaling. Something unfurled in me in response to her kindness. But I knew the darkness was ever-present.

Increasingly, alcohol would lure me to loiter near the edge of death. Even sober, sitting in the unsettling silence of my flat, the thoughts of death would hang over me. I stared over the bannisters down to the ground floor, noticing how steep they were. On a trip to Rome, I looked over a balcony and was disappointed to find it wasn't high enough to kill myself. But picturing my mother receiving the news in a prison cell, I couldn't bring myself to do it. I was trapped in the living with her.

A year after Anthony and I had split up, I tried countering the void by putting myself back on the dating scene. But sooner or later, the inevitable question would arise.

'And what about your parents?'

I could never find the words. But I felt compelled to try and tell the truth.

'He was bad . . .' I would offer in conclusion. 'Controlling . . . he just drove her mad.'

Some would reach out to hold my hand. Others would recoil. But relationships would never last. My grief constantly shifted the ground beneath their feet. Some days I'd be bouncing with excitement for the world. Other days I was mute, curled in a ball on the sofa. And if they somehow managed to survive this, I would find a way to sabotage the relationship before it could grow strong enough to withstand it.

Ultimately, I took up long-term solitude. I knew being alone wasn't good for me, but it became addictive. I craved the peace it offered; it allowed me to feel normal.

The prison doctor eventually prescribed Mum medication for her ups and downs, and her moods settled somewhat. Yet Dad remained her overriding preoccupation. She spoke about him as though he was still here. I couldn't bear it.

During her first year in prison, she had been put on the Freedom Programme, a course which helps teach victims of abuse – and particularly the ones who are not aware that they were victims – about what form abuse takes. The programme presents abusers as three different archetypes: the King of the Castle, the Bully, and the Sexual Controller. I knew nothing about the course until James and I found her frothing with agitation on one of our routine visits.

'I've been on this course,' she said as soon as we sat down. 'And you won't believe it, but everything they were saying, it was about me. And your father. They were just describing everything that happened to me! Everything!'

There was a disbelief, almost horror in her voice as she frantically listed the tell-tale behaviours: the isolating, the financial control, the stonewalling, the denial.

'That's what he used to do to me! Your father, that's exactly how he behaved! I can't believe it!'

'I didn't know that was abuse. I just thought that was normal. Like that time when I made friends with Debbie. Debbie Giles, remember, from antenatal classes. She was coming round for dinner. Your father didn't like me making friends. So he took the pavlova I'd cooked and smashed it on the kitchen floor. *Now you have to cancel*, he said gleefully. Did you know that's something that abusers do?'

Mum's face was amazed. As though it had never occurred to her that this was not normal. I had always thought that Mum knew that Dad's behaviour wasn't right, but she had wanted to stay with him so she accepted it. I realised then it was much simpler than that. She hadn't known that it was wrong. It hadn't occurred to her.

It was too sad to bear – how fragile her life had been. How unprepared she was. My heart broke a little for her and for myself. Because she wasn't the shepherd I had always thought she was. She was a lost sheep.

Chapter Three

By the time Mum had been in prison for about four years, I was gradually finding a better way to exist. My flat in Cricklewood had become my refuge. I found a flatmate, Carlos, the first normal person my age who'd walked through my door. With this new life came a new office job in a small company. It kept me swimming upriver.

I cycled to and from work. The age-old advice of physical exercise, long ignored, now started to take. But still I cycled without a helmet. To take the constant live-or-die decision out of my own hands, to leave it up to fate. But as the years passed, I stayed alive and I realised my path wasn't escape, it was survival. I put on a helmet and a sea of acceptance washed over me. My keel had evened. Structure had found its place in my life.

Then an email arrived from Harriet Wistrich.

A few years earlier, I had been sitting with Mum on a visit when she'd said something that took me by surprise: 'I've got some new lawyers.' Dalla, my cousin's wife, had been a lawyer before having children. She'd told Mum about an organisation called Justice for Women, a feminist campaign group set up to help women who had killed their abusers. The co-founder of the group, which had been going for 23 years by this point, was a lawyer called Harriet Wistrich.

At that point, I had put most lawyers in a file in my brain marked 'not to be trusted'. They represented the system that had not only stripped Mum of her voice, but me of mine too. When an email from Harriet arrived asking to talk, I had wanted to say no. But I accepted.

Days later, I was walking down a scruffy street near Mornington Crescent. I was buzzed into an unassuming entrance in a row of nondescript shopfronts. It felt more like an art studio, with its spacious open-plan layout and warehouse windows – it had no corporate reception or gleam. A small woman, business-like but friendly, greeted me at the door. She was as far away from the stereotypical lawyer as you could get. Short grey hair, everyday clothes and an open manner.

'David,' she said warmly, holding out her hand and smiling. 'Good to meet you. I'm Harriet.'

Harriet asked me about my childhood. What it had been like. What I had seen, what I had heard. She exhumed it all out of me, digging out every detail and gave it air to breathe.

It wasn't like what they said in the trial, the jealousy and rage . . . she was losing her very grip on reality before my eyes.

I found myself talking to her, telling her things in a way I had never done with lawyers before. The shock of reading the legal files had, in the intervening years, lost some of its jagged power. It felt like Harriet was the first person to ask for the full story, not just from my mum's point of view, but from mine too. I appreciated her empathy and her realism. She wasn't full of legal jargon or false confidence. The way she spoke was precise, careful. She was clear about the uphill struggle we would face.

'As you know, in your mum's case it is difficult to find a route to appeal. We would need new evidence,' she admitted.

I left Harriet's office somewhat relieved, but also realistic. I simply couldn't imagine that anything I said could really have helped. The basic fact remained: the evidence hadn't all been used at the trial because nobody wanted to speak ill of the dead and the focus was on the last five years of the marriage, but it wasn't new. All of it had been known at the time.

Over the four years that followed, Harriet got to know my mother quite well, and had asked her to write out her life story. Mum was still going through highs and lows, despite her medication. Some days this task would take her over: she would write reams and reams on endless pieces of paper in a kind of stream of consciousness. On other days, I couldn't even get her to respond to my letters.

Harriet brought another psychiatrist on board to reassess her.

'I'm tired of talking about it, about what had happened, David. The same questions about why I did it. I don't know, I can't access those memories, I don't remember,' Mum would say in exasperation in between her sessions with Dr Gwen Adshead.

'I know, but you have to try. We both have to try.'

The new psychiatrist's evaluation was at odds with what had been said in the first trial. She was diagnosed with a triad of syndromes: manic depression, borderline dependent personality disorder and as bipolar: very different from the diagnosis of depression which had been so endlessly thrashed over in the trial.

*

And then finally, after years of work and disillusionment, a breakthrough came. Harriet was emailing with news. The subject line read: *Sally's appeal.*

Dear All, it opened, *I wanted to let you know we have finally gathered together some new evidence which I believe gives us grounds to argue that Sally's conviction for murder was unsafe.*

The grounds of appeal will involve evidence that Sally was subjected to 'coercive control' by Richard – this is a new statutory definition and understanding of domestic abuse which has only been on the statute book for under a year.

Harriet's email proposed that this new law which encapsulated a better understanding of domestic abuse might assist with the formulation of grounds of appeal, and she and her team were putting together an expert report on the coercive control that Mum had suffered, which, combined with the psychiatric evidence they had gleaned, they would submit to the courts as evidence.

Coercive control? Domestic abuse? What did that mean? To me, the words 'domestic abuse' conjured ideas of men whose wives cowered away from their fists or covered up their bruises with make-up.

After finishing her email, I typed 'Coercive control' into Google. I had barely typed the first letters before it autocompleted and launched me into a forest of articles detailing the previous year's change in the law. Phrases danced in front of my eyes: *a pattern of acts of assault, threats, humiliation and intimidation or other abuse intended to harm, punish or frighten . . . behaviour designed to manipulate how the victim acts, thinks and feels . . . behaving in a way calculated to control.*

Eventually I found my way to the official government website, which defined the new offence in detail, complete with a list of typical behaviours: humiliation, making someone think they are worthless, controlling their money, sexual assault, isolating them from friends and family.

The new law highlighted that each single incident might seem innocent enough on its own, to the extent that victims often don't recognise themselves as victims. If you isolated an incident, it didn't amount to something huge, but if you pulled back and looked at the whole picture, at the pattern building up over time, these fragments became a horrifying mosaic that told the full story of a life twisted by somebody else's will. I looked at the list, ticking off every single point, and vignettes of memory rushed to the surface.

My mother's gaze, fixed imploringly on my father . . .

His head, snapping round to her over the dinner table in anger . . .

The embarrassed silence at parties, his words: 'Thunder thighs . . . you wouldn't want to see her without her clothes on,' falling into dead air . . .

His grin as he stood next to the mantelpiece in the sitting room, a photo of himself with two topless women in his hand . . .

The endless denials about the London Eye tickets. 'You put them there, Sally. You must have put them there yourself!'

The insistent, authoritative voice, again and again over countless arguments: 'You're going mad, Sally. You're making it all up . . .'

The times he had drawn me aside and whispered under his breath to convince me she was drunk . . .

The bend of her head as she abased herself in a pile of phone records . . .

The terrible silence as we drove down that grey LA highway.

I felt lost in a library of memories. Books containing the scenes of my life started flying from shelves all around me, scene after scene falling open, with words engraved on their spines.

MANIPULATION

I'm in the back of a car. I look out as skeins of heather pass me by. *We're in Scotland*, I say to myself. The car starts veering, jolting left-to-right, sharp snaps.

Mum is screaming, 'Richard! What are you doing?! Richard, what's wrong? Why won't you tell me what's wrong!'

She is pleading, begging. *I remember now*, I think to myself, a voyeur to my own memories. *I've never seen her more desperate.*

The silence swallowing us both into submission. Mum's unbearable desperation . . . my eyes squeeze. *I want out of this memory.*

'I'm sorry, Richard. I'm sorry I criticised your driving. I'm sorry.'

I started to see the patterns of acts now. The word ISOLATION gleamed at me.

The time he had struck a pavlova out of her hands and on to the floor rather than let her see her friend . . .

My father banning Jen from the house. Jen, who had always been a mainstay of support to my mother . . .

Another book: HUMILIATION.

Mum on her feet, dancing, her eyes smiling, her joy uncontained, asking Dad to join her. I could still hear my inner thoughts, the way I willed them across the room. *Just one dance, give it to her, Dad, c'mon. Please. Just do it for her, it's the last night, for God's sake!*

And Dad sitting still, unmoving, his own unblinking stare back at her.

Finally, the largest book of them all, its title huge in my mind: COERCIVE CONTROL.

The very words we should have had all along.

Chapter Four

Nothing happened quickly. Two more years ground round before we could even apply for permission to appeal. The long wait didn't surprise me. It was no surprise either when a couple of months later we heard from Harriet that the permission to appeal had been refused.

But Harriet wasn't to be stopped. They were already preparing a new application. This one would be made in person, in a court. This time, the rest of Mum's life would lie in the hands of three judges. And this appeal would be it. You are only allowed to apply twice, and one shot was already gone. If it failed, Mum's life inside would be set in stone for the next twelve years.

Speaking to Mum on the phone later that week, I could hear the disillusionment in her voice.

'I'm sorry, Mum,' I heard myself saying. 'I know it's bad news. But there's one more chance, Harriet says, and you never know.'

Later that night I scrolled back through my emails from Harriet. A line from one of them caught my gaze: 'I think it is worth considering some publicity for this case . . . partly to assist Sally's prospects, and partly to educate the public.'

I could feel something crystallise inside me. The anger I had felt through all these long years began to find a focus. I knew the odds were against her, but if she had one shot left, then this was the moment to do what I could. Whatever happened, I had to know I had done absolutely everything I possibly could to help her. So when Harriet got in touch to say that she wanted one of us to speak at a public meeting that Justice for Women were organising on the subject of women who had killed their violent partners, I said I would.

That night was one of the most terrifying of my life. My hands shook at the lectern with a crowd of well-meaning, well-dressed people standing before me. My vision blurred, my words tangled themselves up as I tried to conjure up a picture of what my childhood was like. The weight of eyes on me was almost too much, until a small woman, realising my distress, came to join me at the lectern, standing side by side with me until I reached the end. It was thanks to her that I got to the end of my speech; only later did I find out it was the distinguished lawyer Baroness Helena Kennedy.

Other requests began to come through via Harriet, until Fiona Hamilton at *The Times* got in touch. I cried in that interview, sitting in the News International offices. I felt an overwhelming pressure to get my words right, long pauses flowering after every question while I worked out how to frame my answer. I was representing not only myself but my mother and my brother too, and I couldn't quell my emotions.

After that, I was caught up in a snowstorm of requests. The big one was the *Today* programme on Radio 4, who wanted to interview Harriet and me together.

I sat on the sofa in my flat, alone, the words glowing up at me from the screen, knowing live radio would put me on the spot in a way that the print interviews hadn't. I wondered if I could hold it together. But then I remembered Harriet's words. *Mum has only one permission to appeal left*, I thought, *and afterwards that's it. No more chances. She'll be in there for the rest of her sentence.*

The realisation came to me: *if I don't do everything I can to make that appeal happen, I won't be able to forgive myself.* With a sinking feeling came a rock-solid certainty: I would do the *Today* programme, and I would also do every single other piece of press that came my way. I typed out my reply. *Yes*, I said, *I'll do it.*

Broadcasting House is an imposing place, with curved stone and glass rising out of the central London streets; an embodiment of the BBC's authority.

'So,' a friendly bearded man said as he checked his clipboard in the lift. 'David Challen, right? You're here to talk about gaslighting, aren't you?'

I looked at him blankly. What was he talking about? Gas? Lighting? My mind touched on blue flames and old lamps.

'Er. My mum's case. Sally Challen? I'm here to talk about coercive control.'

When we got in the recording studio, the interviewer John Humphrys started introducing the first trial's murder verdict and stating that the following week the court of appeal was being asked to rule on whether that conviction should be reduced to manslaughter. Then he turned to me to ask what sort of man my father was.

Then he said, 'How did he treat your mother? What did you see?'

My eyes flicked down my notes. I talked about the

control my mother lived under, how he controlled the whole relationship. I brought up the affairs, the brothels, the casual verbal put-downs and humiliations my dad had dealt out. I could feel my words coming out smoothly enough, the headphones tight against my ears.

Humphrys nodded. Then he turned away from me to Harriet saying, 'but that sort of behaviour, between men and women and sometimes women and men, regrettable though it is, has been around probably forever.'

Harriet's face registered a moment of disbelief before she weighed back in, trying as calmly as she could to convey the complexities of a coercive relationship that had ended in death.

Worse was to come, as Humphrys questioned me, 'if this appeal succeeds, isn't there a danger that it'll send a message that it's all right to kill your husband?'

I sat back as if I had been hit. I felt like he hadn't appreciated what we were trying to convey and there was still so much for people to learn about this hitherto undiscussed subject.

The next request was to do an interview with Stephen Nolan on BBC Radio Ulster. This was going to be a longer interview. By the time I had set myself up in the rear bedroom of my flat, with my headphones on and about eight well-learned pieces of paper spread out in front of me, I felt at least that my feet were on solid ground. We seemed to be skirting round the main issues. Then it hit me: friendly as he was, he wasn't going to ask me the perfect questions. The subject was too new: he just didn't understand coercive control, or the ins and outs of our story. No one did.

I needed to stop being led by what these people asked – it was up to me to tell them what they needed to know. So I took a deep breath, and started to talk.

From that moment on, I gained some measure of confidence. James and I agreed that I should speak for both of us. We would talk the interviews over in advance. Over the next weeks, as I spoke to more and more people, I realised that I needed to give them soundbites about what coercive control is. What it had done to my mother. And why, no, it isn't by any means a licence to kill.

A few weeks later a tabloid ran an interview with me headlined *My Father the Monster.* That word *monster* shouted up at me from the screen. James and I didn't want to verbally tear down our dad in the media. We were prepared to go against our natural instincts, to talk ill of our own father, only when it was necessary. But we didn't want him labelled a monster. We didn't want to set him apart from humanity. I was coming to realise that there were many men like him out there.

We wanted justice for our mother. But we were also our father's sons. We had to tell people who he really was, but also what that had cost him, and cost us.

Interview by interview, I fought to protect our family. I hated listening to my own voice or seeing myself on TV, but I made a concerted effort to listen or watch or read it over once it ran. I had to ensure I was communicating it all correctly. I placed strong restrictions on myself, refusing to allow slip-ups where we were misquoted, and resisting sensationalist headlines. I became obsessive about approval.

*

By now, something impossible had also happened. I had met someone new: John. Tall, blond, with a Belfast accent. The first time we met, our conversation flowed and one drink led to another, which led me back to his flat for more drinks. Sitting in the tiny kitchen, around the even tinier table, he asked the inevitable question.

'So, your parents, what are they like?'

I told him the truth.

It didn't seem to faze him. I hadn't seen that reaction before.

'Jesus, David . . . That's awful. I can't imagine growing up like that. But . . . you know, I thought there was something about you.' He paused. 'We've all got our crosses to bear, haven't we?'

We spoke back and forth about depression. About the things we carried. John, it turned out, had recently surfaced from his own pit of despair, although you wouldn't be able to tell, as he was outgoing, bursting with character and conversation. Yet he too had been fending off his own demons.

John and I saw each other for weeks, which turned into months, and although I tried to sabotage it a few times, he just wouldn't let me. So I allowed him into my life.

Every part of it, barring prison.

I didn't want to take him to that place. I refused to let him walk through all those locked gates and doors, to see Mum sitting there looking small and diminished. That wasn't the mother I wanted him to meet. I wanted him to see the real one, the one I knew, removed from the place that had consumed her identity.

However, as the campaign ramped up, his desire to see her did too. I tried to hold him back. It made me want to fight even more to set her free, believing he could meet her. Away from that place.

'I don't care where she is, she's your mother and I want to meet her. Please?' he would ask and ask and ask.

After 18 months, I knew I had to let him in. By now, my mother had been moved to HMP Send, a state-run prison. It was a big move for her after six years at HMP Bronzefield. It felt foreign and scary. New people, new procedures. High fencing and iron gates, barbed wire running along the top. I shrank into myself, seeing John in a place like this. A dull sense of shame lingered inside me. But he walked right up to my mother and immediately hugged her.

'It's lovely to meet you, John,' she said as the daylight pierced through small, barred windows onto our faces. I felt naked.

'So, Sally. Tell me about the food here. David told me about the cubed chicken and the left drumsticks? Do you still not know where the right legs go?'

She laughed, smiling back at him. 'David never tells me anything about his life, you know,' she said mischievously. 'I ask, but he lets me know very little.'

I listened as John found a way to share what he could of my life, the places we went and the flat we now lived in together, giving Mum a sense of depth to my life that I could not. Seeing them laughing together, my shame thawed.

As we walked away, I looked back to see a look of joy cross her face, her mouth set in something close to her old smile.

Chapter Five

The Court of Appeal in London is nothing like Guildford Crown Court. With its towering gothic arch and pointed turrets reaching to the sky, it is clear that you are at the heart of the British legal system.

It was 1 March 2018.

Having been ground up by the legal system once already, it felt like we were walking back into the pulveriser. A man yelled out to me:

'David! David! Can I get a quick photo please?'

I looked behind me to find a lone photographer who had seemingly been lying in wait, hoping for family members to show up. I didn't know how to react – it was something that had never happened to me before. I looked ahead at Dalla for direction. She gestured for me to do it.

A small number of Justice for Women supporters were already gathered outside, holding placards. *Free Sally Challen!* they proclaimed, under a work profile photo of Mum looking happy, smiling into the lens.

'Can you just stand there and look at the camera please, David?'

The room where Mum's hearing was being held was buried away on the top floor of the building. It was lined in mahogany with a high dais for the three judges. It was like a tomb of judgements, where thousands upon thousands of decisions had been handed down to its prisoners. The dock was almost theatrical, jutting out from the wall and caged in by bars, as though designed for some mythical bird.

It had been determined that my mother would not be attending – not even via video link. She would be waiting to be notified of the verdict from prison. How powerless she must feel, not even allowed to be a spectator at a hearing that would determine the rest of her life.

I was the only immediate family member in attendance. James couldn't face it. The trauma of the first case had left him hopeless.

The mechanisms of the court slowly began to wheeze into life. The clerks of the court scurried beneath the dais in their wigs and gowns amid teetering stacks of papers and files.

This time it is going to be different, I willed in my head. *We know so much more now.*

Our barrister, Clare Wade QC, made the case for the defence. For the prosecution, our old nemesis Caroline Carberry. It felt like watching a prizefight between two boxers. No sooner did one seem to be winning than the opposite would counter-punch.

Back and forth they went, Clare arguing that new evidence about my mother's mental health raised doubts about the safety of her conviction, particularly regarding the impact of coercive control and that bipolar disorder, not considered at trial, which could explain her fluctuating moods. The new psychiatrist's assessment of my mother's history could shed light on her mental state at the time of the offence. This fresh evidence, Clare argued, merited further examination of my mother's conviction. It was based on two strands: first, that the understanding of domestic abuse had changed since the original trial in 2011, and that the case should therefore be reheard in the light of the new legislation. Second, that Mum's original psychiatric diagnosis of depression had been wrong, and that there was now evidence of far more complex disorders which made the original conviction unsafe.

The court broke for the judges to deliberate and everyone filtered out into the foyer. It felt otherworldly; the space was bathed in a soft brightness from an ornate skylight above us. My life seemed to be haunted by these spaces: the family room at Guildford Crown Court, the visitors' hall at HMP Bronzefield, the sparse white surgical room in the mortuary.

'How do you think it's going?' Dalla asked.

'I don't know, it's so hard to tell what the judges are thinking, really. They nod along with Clare one moment, then sound unconvinced by any of it the next.'

When we were called back in, I noticed that the public seats had filled up with journalists, and they were now jostling for seats. The court clerk intoned: 'Family have priority. Any family, please can you make yourselves known!'

One of the three judges, Lady Justice Rafferty, started to speak. I was transported back twelve years, to the moment when Mum had been handed her sentence. My hand gripped the wooden pew beside me. The words continued to unfurl, and nothing she said seemed to contain any hope. Until the very end:

Leave to appeal should be granted.

With those few words, the emotional dam burst inside me. I finally wept, head bowed, tears hitting the court benches, so unlike the verdict all those years ago.

I saw Dalla's eyes overflow with joy. 'We did it!' she said.

I lingered on the benches, collecting myself, a procession of hands patting my back as people filed out past me. I tried to stay grounded, ignoring the furore of excitement I could feel building outside the courtroom. Who knew where this journey was about to take us. This wasn't the end – nowhere near it. This was just the starting gun.

A Radio Five Live van was parked outside the court, and a journalist beckoned me over as I emerged into the cold. I jumped into the van to do a quick interview, trying to marshal my thoughts into coherent sentences.

By now, I was becoming used to the basic shape of the story: the 40 years of dependency Mum had endured, how big a deal it was for her and others that she should be finally recognised as a victim of abuse. But in the short minutes they gave me to speak, I found myself veering off course, lost in the frenetic effort to say the right thing.

'Stop whatever you're doing right now and put your cups of tea down: today is about hope. My mum and our family have finally been heard,' I said joyfully. The journalist looked at me oddly.

As I spoke, I could feel my phone going off in my pocket.

'I'm sorry, I'm going to have to go. My mum is literally calling me!' I said, jumping out of the van.

'It's me, David!' It was as though a completely new tone had crept into her voice – hope, excitement, maybe even a touch of fear. 'Everyone here's so happy for me. You should see it. Everyone's been hugging me and crying, even the warders! I can't believe it. I just can't believe it!'

I was trying to keep up with her, bowled over by the speed of events.

Then her voice dropped a bit.

'I heard you on the radio just now. They allowed me to listen. You were brilliant . . .' I could hear a hesitation in her voice as she continued. 'But I never really knew . . . I didn't know you'd seen and heard so much. I thought I'd kept it from you more.'

'Mum . . .' I couldn't find any words.

What did she mean, she thought I didn't know? Perhaps she had never understood the effect their marriage had had on all of us. I couldn't find the words to explain this to her. Perhaps I never would.

Chapter Six

The bar to getting an appeal hearing was apparently incredibly high. So, to be successful? Harriet's eyes had the look of wing-and-prayer, yet they twinkled back at me with hope. She immediately started building the case and gathering expert testimony. She particularly wanted the evidence of Dr Evan Stark, the American authority on coercive control. His words, she said, would be vital.

The more Harriet explored the legal side of coercive control, the more I sought to learn from domestic abuse charities, services and survivors.

I was already trying to coordinate in my head how to keep interest in my mother's appeal alive. If Harriet was going to be across the legal side, I would do everything I could to be across the media angle and ensure that my mother's cause remained in the public eye until the appeal.

I would have to go much deeper. That meant combing once more through the endless legal files. But now I had more to go on. My mother had written page after page about her life story while in prison, and had also poured her heart out to various psychiatrists. I started to read it all. The real, full story of her life continued to unfold.

At 17, she had became pregnant because Dad didn't believe in contraception. She'd had to have a late-stage termination, a terrible operation that affected her very seriously. Her aunt had had to pay for it, because Dad had refused to, implying that the baby might be someone else's. It had caused such a row that her brothers had gone round to his house to confront him about his behaviour. I remembered all those family gatherings and Christmas parties Dad had refused to attend, and suddenly it all made sense.

The years following the abortion had been lived out on Dad's terms, including a move to Australia, which he had brought her along with begrudgingly. Then a move back into his parents' house, where she was unhappy. A refusal to let her take up a job she was offered. And all through it, he constantly delayed their engagement, despite her longing. When they did get married, he sent her out to buy her own wedding ring. Then began his relationship with another woman, who he used to spend time with around once a week. Mum had confronted him about it. 'Don't make me choose,' Dad had responded. 'Don't make me choose between you and her.'

In the ensuing argument, he had dragged her down the stairs. That altercation had led to my mother's first attempted suicide, with an overdose of aspirin.

When she worked full-time before she had James and me, he had made her hand over her salary. He had kept her so short of money when we were young that she had cleaned Noel's house for extra money to get by. She was made to cook Dad supper every night, and one night he threw the mince she had prepared across the floor.

On one occasion he had looked at her all dressed up and told her: 'I'm not going out with you looking like that.' She'd had to cancel seeing her friend, and for that her friend had never forgiven her. There was even an occasion when he had disabled her car by fiddling with some leads in the engine, to punish her.

The sexual humiliations detailed were nearly too much for me to read about. She had once gone to the doctor's, convinced that something was wrong with her because he said she smelled, intimately. And it seemed that after that first time in LA, he had raped her repeatedly, in the same way as the first time. She hadn't put up any resistance, because she'd hoped that it would make him love her.

Through these details was Mum's constant willingness to do anything for him – to keep the house to his exacting standards and put up with him eyeing up other women in public.

Sometimes on visits to see Mum, I'd try and gather details of her memories, in the hope they'd fill in some gaps. One day, on a whim, I mentioned the family visit to see *Star Wars: The Phantom Menace* – the one she hadn't come on. That memory had always felt slightly off. The feeling of being in the dark of the Leicester Square cinema, Dad beside me, waiting for the film to begin, with a strange feeling that she was alone somewhere else.

'Why weren't you there?' I asked.

She met my eyes for a second then turned away. 'Your dad. It was because of LA.'

The answer lingered between us. A year had passed between that trip and the outing, but still the punishment had continued.

It was reading the new psychiatric reports in full that allowed me to understand her behaviours in conjunction with the control she had been subjected to. Dr Gwen Adshead, the forensic psychiatrist Harriet had brought on board, burrowed right into Mum's history and her episodes in prison, to make sense of how Mum's mind worked. Her diagnosis was that my mother was suffering from personality and bipolar affective disorders. The spike in frenetic behaviour she had shown in recent years was an indicator of these conditions existing well before she had been in prison.

On top of that, her findings showed the impact that the years of coercive control had had on Mum. 'If a partner also treats them in a derogatory or coercive way, then this may paradoxically strengthen the attachment to the coercive partner,' she explained. It seemed unfathomable, but Dad's behaviour had worked on Mum not to make her love him any less, but to strengthen her dependence.

The report from the coercive control expert, Dr Evan Stark, best described it all. It gave a shape to what had seemed always an indefinable fog to me.

He went through all their history, building up a pattern of incidents and showing how Mum had been shaped by Dad's will for so long – through control, through sexual humiliation, through fear – that she had 'internalised' his rules for living. She 'lived under his shadow'.

So many lines jumped out at me, colouring in the contours of what I had only glimpsed as a child. How he had stopped her seeing old friends. How he had withheld her money. How he had dominated and degraded her.

And how he had once demanded that she go out with him and some friends when her mother was dying in a nursing home. That one broke my heart.

You could describe it as my father 'grooming' my mother for 'dependence'.

Even when they had separated, she was trying to bend her life to his shape: still letting him rule her head when it came to who she should see, how she should dress, even what meals she should prepare. She had built up a model of him in her head – what Dr Stark called an 'imago', and still lived her life according to his wishes. That was what had led her back into his orbit.

'However badly he made her feel about herself,' the report said, 'it was better than feeling like nothing, which is how she felt without him.' And by going back she had agreed to live entirely on the terms he had set out for her, however unfair they were. She just had not been able to understand the psychological cost to herself. With his final deception – and even worse, with the realisation that she wasn't allowed to question him about it – came the understanding that she wasn't even allowed to assert her own reality. It was this that finally broke her in two. 'When she struck, it was with the cumulative rage of 30 years of hurt,' the report said.

I had long believed that my mother was no longer fully a person by the end. I hadn't known how to express that or explain it, but finally I understood the pressures that had caused her to crack. How she had not been able to consider the psychological cost of trying to reconcile with my father. She had lived her life in a world that my father had created for her since she was 15 years old. But his lies had finally broken the fabric of that world. Even after years of being told she was going insane, she had tried and tried to claw her way to the truth, by trying to find out what was really going on, by going over and over it with everyone she could speak to. She had been scratching away at it to try and find solid ground from which to leave him forever.

I remembered the words she had uttered in distress to the police team that had talked her down from Beachy Head.

'If I can't have him, no one can.'

The words of a woman on the precipice of death, trying to find her way back to the world he had built for her.

I felt myself drop to the ground as I read, the folder still open in my hands. For so many years I had clawed for a way to explain the inexplicable.

And here it finally was.

Finally, someone gets it.

Chapter Seven

Justice for Women was a small, unfunded campaign group, and they had no press person to dedicate to us. Instead, I had to learn to coordinate it all myself, on top of my office job. I became obsessed with learning how the minds of journalists and programme editors worked.

It was a strange equation: at the same time as I was educating myself, I was having to educate others. This subject was still so new that people in the wider world, including the media, were still learning about it. It wasn't a simple thing to communicate – there was no one headline-grabbing soundbite I could give. Whenever I was asked for an example of coercive control, I could feel myself inwardly stifling my exhaustion: there was never enough time, never enough space to get it exactly right.

Interviewers would tend to fix on one thing. Your mum did this terrible thing, they would say. How was that justified? They wanted one neat example of abuse to justify her extreme reaction. But, of course, I couldn't give it to them – there was no smoking gun, but a series of deep psychological interactions that worsened over the years, until they were so ingrained they lost their definition.

But what really opened my eyes were the connections I was forming with other survivors and activists as the campaign gathered pace. For decades, there had been an ongoing struggle to bring recognition of coercive control to light, but now the emergence of the new law created a groundswell of stories that needed to be shared.

Invitations poured in for me to attend more conferences and meetings with charities and specialist services, which gave me the opportunity to speak with many more survivors.

I was beginning to realise how widespread the tentacles of abuse and control were.

This was made physically clear to me when I was invited to speak at a conference for the domestic abuse charity Women's Aid. I was one of only two men in the entire audience. Sitting at the back as woman after woman spoke up, I realised that this was a safe sanctum for women imprinted with the violence of men.

It was an arresting awakening.

By the time I was called to give my own speech, the pristine sheets I held were crumpled as I clutched them in fear, terrified of taking up too much of these women's time.

I read my speech as fast as I could, trying to wrap things up quickly. But when I glanced up towards the end, I realised the faces looking at me were attentive, sympathetic. I felt not just heard, but understood. Afterwards, so many people expressed gratitude that I as a man was speaking up about this.

I was incredibly gratified, but also confused. Why was I being thanked for the simple act of talking about what we had been through?

Over and over, through the months to come, I heard from women how control defined both their physical and their mental realities. How they had become isolated from friends and family, how they were told how to look, talk and behave. When they should be home. How they had been trained to walk on eggshells. Their home a prison, their abuser their warden. How their finances were controlled, leaving them tied to debts or trapped in homes. How their movements were tracked with technology. How coercive control permeated and destroyed every part of their lives and free will.

Over time, I took on their stories, carrying them within me. One day, a woman beckoned me over.

'I found myself there, David,' she said, gripping my arm. She pulled me in closer, her voice lowered. Fear radiated from her. 'I stood at the foot of his bed and looked down on him. I felt myself falling away, like I was losing myself, David . . .' she trailed off, then took a breath. 'I could have killed him, I felt it . . . I know where your mother's been.'

Her eyes pierced into mine. Her lips folded. A familiarity about her face struck me cold. It was like looking at my mother. It was the first time a survivor had shared with me that she was close to killing her abuser, but it wasn't the last. It was a deathly reminder of what was at stake. This would happen again.

Countless other stories showed me that institutions like the police, judiciary and the courts all failed to grasp an understanding of coercive control. The worst accounts I heard came from the survivors who had been dragged through the family courts. They detailed how their children had been used by their abusers as pawns, to coerce and control and ultimately poison them against the victim. Sometimes those stories did take root in their children's hearts, leaving them convinced that their mothers were unwell, or worse, liars.

'My adult son doesn't believe me, David. He believes I'm making it all up,' one lady told me. Her face was forlorn, existing beyond the edges of hope. Others were in the middle of it, battling not to lose their children.

'He knows every lever to pull, every single one, and no one can see what's he doing,' another lady told me, exasperated. 'If I try to tell them, they say I'm poisoning them, David.'

Dad's voice echoed in my ears: 'You've poisoned my children against me.'

It made me angry, for all of us.

One day, I received a Facebook message from my old guitar teacher, Owen. I hadn't heard from him since our last lesson at Ruxley Ridge.

'David,' it said. 'I'm so pleased to see you speaking out for your mother. I remember when I used to teach you at your house. There was an uncomfortable atmosphere that I could feel in your home. If there's anything I can do to support, please let me know.'

The memories all rushed back to me. Owen and me standing in the playroom, making small talk, his expression uncomfortable, as though he just wanted to leave. *Was the atmosphere in my home really that noticeable?* I thought.

Every person who joined us on the campaign felt like another steam engine attaching itself to our ever-growing train, pushing us to the summit of this Goliath-like mountain.

It was during this time that I reached out to my local MP, Dawn Butler, who passed the case on to the Deputy Leader of the Welsh Labour party, Carolyn Harris. She was incredibly warm, inviting me to Portcullis House to meet her, and even visiting my mum in prison.

And then we upped the stakes by deciding to take part in a BBC documentary. The idea was originally mooted by a producer, who'd got in touch via Harriet and wanted to use our story as a way to explore the new law.

It was a terrifying prospect. As a family, we agonised over this. The memories of our first exposure to the media – those blaring headlines and intrusive pictures – had never faded. Inviting the cameras into our day-to-day lives, for good or ill, was a huge step. We would be laying ourselves wide open, and without any real control over how they would portray Mum.

The hardest person to get on board was James, who was incredibly suspicious of the media. I talked him into it eventually – and if it went wrong, it was on me.

So we let the filmmakers right into our lives. For months, we spent hundreds of hours with them endlessly filming. The novelty soon wore off. They filmed me running around a park on a cold Saturday morning. I didn't run usually, but they told me to get some atmospheric shots.

The producers came to me one day with the idea of filming me looking at Ruxley Ridge, at Ashton Place, and finally at Dad's grave. That gave me pause. I hadn't been back to that graveyard since the funeral. I felt guilty about it, but I couldn't bear to make the trip alone, and I couldn't bear bringing anyone with me. Now, though, was the time.

It was a bright, wintry day, the bare branches making the graveyard even starker. I couldn't seem to get my bearings as I walked between the graves. We hadn't put up a headstone, so I wasn't sure what I was looking for. Dad had been on his own when we buried him, but now there were rows of neatly kept graves all around him. And then I saw it: 'Richard Arthur Challen. Died 15 August 2010. Aged 61 years.' Someone had put up a little wooden cross with a small brass plaque at its heart.

There was no moment of revelation. I looked down, and then crouched closer to the earth he lay in. I touched the grass softly, hoping to grieve. I had expected to cry, but I just felt a numb kind of emptiness. A sadness for him, that this was where he had ended up. Sadness that we had so little connection. Sadness that it had ended this way.

'If he was still here, what would you have said to him? Could you have made him see what he was doing was wrong?' the producers asked me a few moments later.

I considered it, realising how much I wished I had had that opportunity. Could I possibly have managed to show him what he was doing? Could he look past the man I was today and still see 'little David'?

But death is the end of all conversations, and any answers lay silenced somewhere under that modest wooden cross.

The date set for the appeal raced towards us. It had been a year of constant focus. Now that I had the media's attention, it was up to me to keep it on us. I was endlessly trying to build interest in the appeal date, to rally as many people as I could to the cause.

By now, my activity had become almost feverish. I had lined up as much publicity as possible for the week of the appeal, trying to ensure maximum coverage. Less than two weeks before, I was sitting at my desk at work when I received an email from Harriet. The date had been pushed back 'owing to judicial availability'. I stood up, fighting tears. Everything had been leading to this day, and suddenly it had disappeared over yet another horizon. I felt dangerously close to the edge, unable to take any more setbacks.

A new date was set: 27 and 28 February. That morning I went on *Good Morning Britain*. The BBC documentary camera crew filmed me as I appeared on the show. I looked greyed-out with exhaustion, a reflection of how I felt inside. A hollow shell, trying to emote the story one last time. A year of bleeding myself dry for the media, giving as much as I could. This day would be the end of it all.

Chapter Eight

The day of the appeal hearing.

Journalists had often teased me with questions about the prospect of us winning. 'What's the first thing you'll do if she comes out?' But for the last year I hadn't let myself think for a moment past this day. There was a palpable commotion from the crowd gathered outside the Court of Appeal as we approached. I had put a call out on social media to get as many people to the court as possible. A BBC camera interrogated every inch of my face from the passenger seat as we drew closer to the drop-off point.

It was the placards I saw first: a sea of Mum's face framed by a black background, all waving at me. A surreal welcome. *Free Sally!* proclaimed an enormous banner.

We were out in force: John and me, James and Jen, Terence and Nigel, Hugo and Dalla, Noel, my other cousins, our old neighbour Jack Cowdy. And, of course, Harriet, her partner Julie – a gregarious force of nature and co-founder of Justice for Women – along with other campaigners from the group. Carolyn Harris the MP was there, and some of the other survivors I had got to know along the way. I was walking along the banner, greeting everyone who stood behind it, when suddenly I came upon my old guitar teacher, Owen, holding aloft a placard with my mum's face on it. I couldn't believe he had come all this way. Then it dawned on me as his eyes caught mine, and we exchanged a knowing nod: he felt something too.

The wood-panelled main room in the Court of Appeal seemed different from any of the other courts I'd visited over these years – more alive somehow. We'd had to be moved to the biggest courtroom in the building because so many people wanted to come. The sprawling benches of public gallery in front of us and the vast balcony above it were packed. Many visitors were turned away. There was a wall of chatter and support behind us, making it feel more like an amphitheatre than a court. It wasn't just us versus the Crown today, it was everyone behind us against them. We were here for justice.

I took a deep breath as we made our way in. A spot had been saved for me on the end of one of the benches near the front, beneath a large video screen. I looked back to see the rest of the family seated just a few rows behind. James was sitting on his hands, hunched ever so slightly forward.

This time, Mum would be appearing on a large screen, and I would be able to see her clearly. The screen flicked on and a small room appeared. A door opened. Mum walked in and sat down in front of the camera, a female guard standing at her side.

A ripple of hushed discussion moved across the gallery. I realised that this was the first time they'd been able to see the woman she had become in prison. The photos in the media were of a well-presented, happy woman in nice dresses and smart suits. On the screen now was the mother James and I knew, dressed in a grey tracksuit.

The proceedings started with ceremonials and opening statements. I could see that Mum was having trouble following what was going on. She peered into the camera, squinting and straining to hear. She was there to see justice served, but could barely watch it play out.

In the central seat of the three judges presiding over it all was Lady Justice Hallett. She was a no-nonsense woman with a fierce blonde bob and pearl earrings, all topped off with the wig and black gown of justice, and a pair of reading glasses perched on the bridge of her nose.

Clare Wade, our barrister, stood first. She was business-like and calm as she explained the concept of coercive control, citing the evidence of Dr Evan Stark as well as the revised diagnoses of psychiatric disorders. She pointed out the pattern of abuse that Mum had been subjected to, and the manic episodes she'd had in prison, and how these pointed to disorders that had been present at the time of the incident.

Lady Hallett kept returning to the issue of coercive control, her questions sceptical. Calmly, Clare explained once again how it fit into the puzzle.

A ripple of unease spread across the room. We had two strands to our argument: Mum's mental state, and the new statute of coercive control. I wasn't sure they were landing. I could see Harriet fidgeting in her seat. But Lady Hallett wouldn't relent. Her stern words sliced through the hush of the courtroom:

'You can't just say that if you are the victim of coercive control, that gives you a defence. It doesn't.'

Then Caroline Carberry harked back to the question of the hammer. Why was the hammer in Mum's bag? Why had she brought it along? It seemed to me she was finding a kind of relish in describing the ugly details, over and over again.

Then she argued that Mum had been working competently at her job so couldn't have been mentally unwell. She had made the same argument in the first trial. But this time gasps of disgust filled the courtroom. This time it was being received in horror by the spectators, not with passive acceptance. The judge had to rein the spectators in more than once, such was the level of support in court for Mum's case. Dr Gilluley, the psychiatrist for the prosecution, now agreed with Dr Adshead that she had a trio of different disorders. He took to the stand.

The defence and prosecution took their final turns at the stand. There was little for us to cling to in the way of hope. Lady Justice Hallett seemed to be unpicking some of our arguments and casting parts of it aside.

'As you know, this case has received a great deal of public attention. There may be people out there who think this is all about coercive control, this appeal. It's not,' she stated.

'No,' Clare quickly replied, in agreement.

'Primarily, it's about diagnosis of disorders that were undiagnosed at the time of the killing, at the time of the trial,' Lady Justice Hallett went on.

Clare responded: 'Yes, which in wider terms, may or may not be the consequences of the harm that is caused by coercive control.'

My ears pricked up. *Was she helping Clare's argument?*

Lady Justice Hallett leaned forward, pausing momentarily with her lips pursed.

No one dared utter a word.

'Right,' she finally said.

The judges then retired to consider their verdict, to be announced at 2.30 that afternoon.

As I tried to collect my thoughts in the corner of the pub Justice for Women had rented out, a voicemail popped up on my phone: Mum.

'I'm not sure that it's going very well. I don't know, what do you think? I don't know . . .' She sounded defeated.

2.30pm approached, time somehow racing and dragging at the same time. We filed back into court. As I took my seat, the BBC documentary director, Rowan, tried to hook me up with a mic so that she could record my immediate reaction. I resigned myself to her. From the seat next to me, John looked across with a flash of steel. He shook his head. Somehow, though, it happened anyway.

Then Lady Justice Hallett started to speak. I was sitting at the end of the front pew, right next to the monitor showing Mum's face. She was peering into the camera, her confusion once again evident. Would she even be able to hear her fate?

'It is important to remember that coercive control is not a defence to murder,' Justice Hallett explained before she then began to talk about Mum's psychiatric assessment and how 'it is in that context that the theory of coercive control may be relevant'. I clung tightly to the bench in front of me; my knuckles had become translucent orbs.

'We are satisfied therefore that it does undermine the safety of that conviction. We shall quash that conviction.'

She had thrown out the murder conviction.

I didn't break my position, still holding onto the wooden

pew. I wasn't ready to celebrate yet. I wanted to hear her be set free.

'. . . the only proper option for us is to order a retrial.'

I had never thought that this would be the result. In my mind, it had been binary: yes or no. Murder or manslaughter. Everyone around me was celebrating this landmark moment. Relief was written all over Harriet's face. I sat slumped. All I could think of was the idea of having to go through a trial all over again. John looked over at me and knew immediately how I felt.

'I can't . . . I can't go through this again,' I said. 'I don't have any more energy, I can't.'

I looked at my mother on the screen, and she was just as dazed as I was.

It didn't feel like a victory. Noticing me paralysed, Harriet came over to rally me. 'Look at what we've achieved, David.' she said. 'We quashed her murder conviction. What we have won is seismic, not just for us, but for countless other victims of abuse.'

She was right. My tears began to fall. I knew this victory was huge, Goliath even, in what it meant for us and every other victim of coercive control. It had raised an awareness of coercive control in every corner of the country. But deep down, I was begging for the end. Oh, how I wished it would all end.

Outside there were banks of photographers all angling for a shot of this landmark occasion under the bright sun. 'Say how you feel,' Harriet warned as we walked out, 'but you need to be careful. As the case is sub judice [under judicial consideration] now, there are reporting rules.'

I kept it short, feeling my voice wavering as I spoke.

As sons, we get another shot for our story to be heard, for our mother to have another shot at freedom – a freedom she has never had since the age of 15.

I was in a reflective mood in the pub afterwards, as I drank with Harriet and the Justice for Women supporters. I was beginning to accept the measure of what we had achieved together. What Harriet had done for us was immeasurable: she had delivered a voice not just for us, but countless other victims of coercive control. She had breathed a future into my family's lives. Mum may have still been behind bars, but she was no longer a murderer. No one could say that any more.

I stirred awake at Hugo's the next day to buzzing and pinging from my phone. Anyone who had my number was messaging me. Old school friends, ex-colleagues, people I had barely interacted with outside of chance meetings, all of them reaching out, overjoyed. Online, the messages were in their thousands, from survivors of abuse and victims trapped in abusive relationships, to the general public and Mum's ex-prison officer at HMP Bronzefield, who'd always believed she deserved to be free.

I was prepared for the outpouring of sadness for what Mum had had to endure, but the acknowledgement of what I had been through too, all those years of walking alone in darkness, shook me. I was particularly touched by the many messages from people who knew what it meant to be a child witnessing abuse. One lady, also from Claygate, messaged me to say that her childhood was blighted by psychological violence, attesting to the reality that abuse can exist anywhere – even behind the closed doors of middle-class, leafy suburban households. Another spoke about the pin-drop silence in her family home.

Newspapers were strewn across the table downstairs, Mum's smiling face splashed across the front pages. I felt like a child on a Christmas morning. I grabbed the first paper, *The Daily Telegraph*:

JUDGES GIVE HOPE TO WOMEN WHO KILLED ABUSIVE HUSBANDS

Looking across the images of her in the papers, it was as though they had magically changed. The tinge of sadness that had always seemed washed across them had disappeared, as though they had come back to happy life. Mum was my mum again.

But the weeks ahead were filled with a feeling of impotence. Now that we were heading for a retrial, reporting restrictions applied to the case. I had lost my ability to speak out in the media. It was distressing to be silenced again, though the petition we had put out, to raise awareness for the disparity of treatment of women tried for violent crimes against that of men for similar, was racking up thousands of signatures. The petition called on the Crown Prosecution Service to drop the murder charge against Sally Challen, arguing that forcing her to undergo another trial was not in the public interest.

By the end of March, Harriet emailed the family to confirm that she had made an application for bail. The psychiatrists had confirmed Mum did not pose any danger and supported her application. James would be made one of the sureties, responsible for Mum and for providing a safe place for her to stay should she get out.

The Crown Prosecution Service were opposing the bail application, just as we had anticipated. I was incensed with rage that they would deem a 64-year-old woman, with no previous history of violence, such a risk to society as to oppose her bail.

We had to weigh up whether Mum wanted to be at court, or to appear via video link. If she came to court and was denied bail, she'd risk losing her cell. 'Prison is hell,' Mum would regularly tell us, 'but that cell is my home.' We agreed that she should appear via video link.

Come April, we went to the Old Bailey, where Lord Justice Edis granted the application with little concern, noting that the trial would begin on the 1 July – 'if there was to be a trial'. For eight years, seeing Mum had meant guards and waiting rooms, a noisy hall and fluorescent lights. And now she would simply be among us, staying with James like any other mother might.

It might not be forever, but we would have her home. Tomorrow.

She was going to come out.

Chapter Nine

I seemed to float through the barriers at the station on the way back from the Old Bailey. Mum would be back tomorrow. Just as I was glancing up at the train indicator, my phone buzzed. I didn't recognise the number. 'Hello, is that David Challen? I'm calling from the Old Bailey. There's a last-minute change. Your mother can be released today. If you can get to the prison now, you can collect her.'

'Right now, you mean?'

'Right now, yes.'

The prison closed at 5pm. It was 3pm.

Heart racing, I called James.

'James, have you heard? Where are you?'

'We're on our way home. What's wrong?' His voice was confused, caught up in my panicked excitement.

'The court just called me to say they can release her NOW. We can pick her up NOW.'

'What?! Are you sure?'

'Yes! I called the prison to check. I'll meet you there.'

Then I careened up the escalators at Waterloo, running full pelt the whole length of the station concourse to the platform. I made it by seconds.

At the prison, we were greeted by the familiar faces of the staff at the visitors' centre who we had got to know over the years. But this time, they didn't just wave us on to the main building. We all understood that the judge's decision to rush the release through was to help us avoid the media.

'OK, so, what we'll do is, we're going to let you drive your car in, through the main gates. You can pick her up from there.'

We all looked at each other, shocked. Pete, the guard with whom we regularly bantered, confirmed our suspicions.

'I've been here for God knows how long, and this never happens,' he marvelled.

They swung open the huge, solid double gates. We laughed at the absurdity of what was happening, and drove through. The gates slowly closed behind us as the guards asked us to step out of the car to conduct a thorough search. They scoured every part they could access, lifting up floor mats and the engine hood.

Then we got back in the car and the next double gates opened. We drove into a large area in front of the main building and parked next to a long wire fence, under the gaze of hundreds of tiny cell windows. We waited, staring at the small door leading into the main building. And then the door opened, and we saw her. It was as though she was moving in slow motion. A tiny little figure on a long, slow walk towards us. She was carrying every single one of her possessions in big plastic bags: nine years of her life, bundled up in her arms.

All three of us were crying as she came towards us – even the prison guards were trying to compose themselves. Then she was right in front of us and we were hugging and crying, crying and hugging. And even though this was all happening under the eyes of the guards, it felt like a prison break as we climbed in and drove back through the gates and out into the world.

Mum was calling everyone she knew as we sat in traffic on the M25.

'Christopher! Guess where I am?'

'Terence, you'll never guess what I'm doing!'

'I'm stuck in traffic on the M25. Isn't it brilliant!'

'It's the first and last traffic jam she'll actually enjoy,' Jen said.

It was like we'd just pulled off a heist. We were giddy, convinced that any moment someone would catch us up and take her back. Mum was talking nineteen to the dozen: 'They were all watching out the windows, all the other prisoners, you know. They were so happy for me. It was so nice . . . like something in a movie.'

Then came the strangeness of letting her into the house. It was like an anthropological experiment. We watched her feel her way through these everyday rooms, exclaiming about the things that were familiar and the things that weren't. We fussed around her as though she was an infant, unable to let her out of our sight. I'd catch myself standing back and looking at her in disbelief from a distance. She'd return a reassuring smile back at me. *Yes*, it said, *I am here. This is happening.* Then I'd hug her, to make double sure this was all real.

There was the question of what to have for supper – a seemingly tiny but truly momentous decision. She chose Indian, and ate every mouthful with an extraordinary relish, savouring the chutneys and the poppadoms. I remembered all those phone calls over the years, her need to imagine foods that were unreachable to her. A glee spread across her face as she realised she could have Indian any time she liked.

The next day, I filmed her in Marks & Spencer. Every moment witnessing her doing anything, even if it was mundane, was special – none of it seemed real. She just smiled and laughed at everything. 'Look, do you remember those?' she said, pointing at a box of profiteroles. I knew we were remembering the days when she used to make my favourite dessert from scratch: the choux pastry, whipped cream and her own rich chocolate sauce.

I even filmed her having a sip of her first hot chocolate in years, a childlike wonder overtaking her at the richness of the taste. She held still, as if to pose for a photo.

'It's a video, Mum,' I said.

She laughed, her eyes smiling at the technology. She hadn't really seen a smartphone before.

There were the things that had bypassed her in prison; things like apps and emojis were an alien language to her. It was as though she had been frozen in time. But within days of getting a phone, she was sending WhatsApps festooned with emojis and GIFs.

'Mum, how do you know how to use a poo emoji?' I asked, having received a deluge of texts from her at work.

'James taught me!' she replied.

James and I were both aware that all of this excitement came with a huge amount of responsibility. It wasn't all going to be easy. Returning to us after almost a decade in prison, she had multiple mental disorders and would require immense care.

As the days passed, family flocked from across the country to see her. Every hug with her brothers was protracted and meaningful. Many of them had faced the thought that they wouldn't be alive to see her set free.

We took her for a Sunday roast in a pub, something that had seemed like a wild fantasy only months before. We were playing at being the normal family. I glanced up through the window when James and Mum went outside to have a smoke, and saw her gathering him into a hug, the two of them laughing. The most mundane scene in the world, the most precious.

Yet we all knew that she was out on bail, not free. That meant she had to remain at James's place, and be in the house from 6pm. When the police knocked on the door, she had to be there to answer it. On other days she would have to check in at the local police station.

At last, John and I fulfilled what had been a fantasy of mine throughout all the years I had visited her in jail: a day out in London. As John and I walked her around the city, it became apparent that Mum was a lot older now, unable to walk long distances without stopping. A reminder of the time that had been stripped from us.

As she slowed down, growing tired again, we sat on a bench near London Bridge, looking out across the Thames.

'Sally, would you often get to see much of the outside world when you went on hospital visits out of prison?' John asked.

'Oh, yes,' she said. 'You'd get to sit in normal places with the public, see the world go by, but you'd always be handcuffed to a guard.'

She got up and walked over to the barrier, looking across the river at the city, exercising the freedom she now had to move, unchained. She turned back and looked at me, smiling.

But then there was the final rush for the train, to get home in time for her curfew. We wondered if we were living on borrowed time.

Chapter Ten

A few months before the retrial date, Sarah – the original FLO who had been with us on the very first day – sent a message to James and me, asking for a meeting with the detective in charge of the case. They had important news, she said. That was all.

We quickly realised that they wanted to see us, not Mum, because they were talking to us as the children of the victim. Mum wouldn't be allowed to be present.

I sat staring at my phone long after the message arrived, my heart racing. I knew what this could mean, but I didn't let myself believe it. Not yet.

As part of the preparations for the retrial, Mum had had to see another forensic psychologist who was assessing her on behalf of the CPS. Harriet had made it clear that he would be key to whether they believed they had the evidence to take her back to trial for murder. Mum had returned from the meeting unsettled. She couldn't quite explain why, something about his tone, the way he had spoken to her. She looked pensive. There was nothing said outright, but she felt something had shifted, or maybe that was just what she wanted to believe.

It stirred something in all of us. A hysteria of hope. We clung to the judge's parting words months earlier when he granted her release: 'if there was to be a trial'. That 'if' had become a carrot since Mum had returned. And now, this message.

Harriet tried to steady us, reminding us not to get ahead of ourselves. Not to hold on too tightly.

It was a spring morning when Sarah and the detective came to my flat bearing a letter. I kept pleasantries to the point: I found it difficult to be welcoming to them. They, who, I believed, were part of an unjust system that had portrayed my mum as a jealous, vengeful murderer. I was no longer that fearful and vulnerable 23-year-old man caught in the throes of a disaster he didn't understand. I was wide awake.

Sarah opened the letter and read it aloud. It was an explanation to me, as the son of the victim, that the CPS was intending to withdraw their charge of murder. Instead, a manslaughter plea would be accepted at the next hearing, when a judge would resentence her accordingly, taking into account the time she had already spent inside.

I knew from Harriet that due to the time Mum had already served, a manslaughter verdict would mean she would be free.

It was done.

The relief came with a deep ache of rage. It wasn't what I wanted to feel, but as I sat there, all I could think of was my twenty-three-year-old self, curled up on Noel's sofa, watching Sarah walk in. To me they were part of a system that saw my mother as nothing more than a woman who had killed her husband. It was then that I realised my mum, Sally Challen, would never truly get to tell her side of the story in a legal setting. I'd long since accepted that Mum's freedom rested on her being labelled mad, rather than bad. But there was little truth behind that verdict – little of the real, full story. Mum was primarily a victim of coercive control, which I felt had prompted a series of mental health disorders. The system wouldn't learn from this.

The final court date was 7 June 2019.

This was another hearing for the prosecution to state their intent: whether to pursue a murder retrial. Gathering that day, round the corner from the Old Bailey, we all had a secret no one knew: that they would not pursue a retrial and our mother was about to be set free. They had already told us they would accept Mum's manslaughter plea. The hearing would then become a resentencing, based on her new conviction. We knew she had served more time than any likely sentence. She would walk free. But until the judge spoke, none of us could fully breathe.

James, Jen, John, my mother and me had one last huddle, and then we strode in, knowing this was our last day in court. The media and journalists set up outside had no idea of what was about to happen. To them, this was just another hearing.

The main players were all there. Harriet and Clare, as well as Caroline Carberry, campaigners, activists, journalists who supported us, journalists who traumatised us. They were all here for it.

My mother had to go back into the dock for one last time, to hear the final sentence given officially.

For one final time we heard the devastating events read back to us at length.

Mum was pronounced guilty of manslaughter rather

than murder, for reasons of diminished responsibility. She was given a sentence of 14 years, automatically reduced by a third because she had always admitted she killed him. She had already served her sentence, said the judge.

Entitled in law to be released at once.

As the judge adjourned, I saw Mum still sat in the dock, looking ahead, lost. I think she was awaiting the instructions of the guard, out of habit. I stormed up to the side door and angrily asked for her to be let out. She wasn't a prisoner any more, and I didn't want her to be in there a moment longer. They unlocked the door and I helped her out.

She was free.

The family gathered at the entrance to the court, facing another bank of photographers before walking to the press conference. The path was lined with throngs of supporters and activists, people who knew what this ruling meant. We moved through a swarm as if on a pilgrimage, camera shutters clicking all around us and fuzzy microphones hovering in the air above. Mum delivered a speech she had written. She thanked everyone: her family, Harriet, Justice for Women, the prison staff, all the members of the public who had supported her. But above all she acknowledged all her fellow victims of coercive control serving time for murder when it should have been manslaughter. 'I know those women are there, because I've met them,' she said.

My eyes welled up with tears of pride. How far she had come from the grey, compliant woman beaten down by a life of abuse and lost in a criminal justice system. Here she was speaking her powerful truth to the world: her case was not unique, and there were many more women just like her.

Chapter Eleven

This should have been our happily ever after. Roll the credits. Splice in a montage of Mum living a normal life: pottering in a sunlit garden, cooking in a bright kitchen.

But things are never that easy.

Prison had made Mum dependent and unable to cope on her own. She would sit around all day, drinking, watching TV and smoking. Her hand was permanently attached to a vape, which a friend in prison had given to her before they separated. If she wasn't vaping, she was smoking, and with that came a horrendous cough and a quiet wheezing when she breathed. We were already hyper-conscious of the time she had lost, and the sight of her with a cigarette in her hand, careless about her own health, felt like an unravelling rope.

Mum tried living with James and Jen, but this quickly became a huge strain on them. She didn't know how to leave them alone. I think she assumed she would resume her role as matriarch. Her life before she went inside had been spent running a household, catering to Dad's every demand. Now, there was nobody who relied on her.

As she settled into her newfound freedom, her mood became hyper, almost manic. She would dart about the home, talking at a million miles per hour. She wanted to do everything and anything, now.

'Oh, can we go and buy some cheese? I want to get some cheeses! Oh, we need to get some plants for your garden. I'll plant them today. Cardigans, I need some cardigans. Can we pop down to M&S?'

Worse was the intense pendulum swing of her emotions. Left-to-right, up-and-down, we couldn't keep up.

'Mum, slow down. Not everything needs to be done today,' I would say, hoping she would slow down. 'Just breathe, you're sounding really hyper.'

My eyes darted to James, in concern. We had seen this behaviour, these swinging highs and lows, years before in prison. She needed support, and since her release neither the prison service nor the criminal justice system who entrusted her back to us gave us any instruction on how to handle this. I had expected it might happen. I had learned along the way that the justice and prison systems consistently failed women. They often leave prison destitute, and many are not offered support to tackle the root causes of their offence, and a huge percentage of women offenders have experienced domestic abuse.

'Mum, are you taking any medication?' I finally asked.

'I'm fine, please don't worry,' Mum replied. 'Of course I'm excited, I just got out of prison!' But after weeks of pleading, she eventually agreed to see a GP.

I had long feared how my mother would cope in a world without my father. Though she was no longer behind bars, I now came to fear that she wasn't free in her mind; that she was still locked away in the prison Dad had built for her. I thought of the police interview in which she admitted to considering suicide on multiple occasions. 'I wasn't supposed to be here,' she had said. 'I was supposed to have jumped, so Richard and I could be together somewhere else.'

She was still obsessed, still wore her wedding ring. She would bring him up out of nowhere. Almost anything might set her off. Sometimes it would be fond, more often accusatory. It was her insistence on using the phrase 'your father' that particularly tore. Dad was her husband in good memories, and 'your father' in the worst ones.

We'd had years and years of living in the world without Dad, but for her, it was as though time had frozen, and she was only just beginning the mourning process. And her return carried an unsettling weight, forcing us to confront his absence all over again.

This was hard to deal with for all of us, and we were also worried about the release of the BBC documentary.

We didn't know what effect all this would have on Mum. I saw the documentary on my own a couple of weeks before its release, in a private screening room. I walked the streets of Soho later in a daze, disappointed by what I had seen. The documentary didn't widen out the general subject of coercive control at all and seemed, at times, to be very focused on the sensational side of Mum's story. It had left a lot of the emotional content – the hours of interviews we had subjected ourselves to – out of the picture.

It was decided that Mum should speak to the media for the first time, on her own terms. Mum said she was happy to do it, so I set up interviews and helped connect her with journalists and news programs I trusted. I did everything I could to make sure they recognised her fragility, and to ensure they gave her a duty of care. As the week of interviews approached, I remained by her side. I sat in the green rooms and to the side of the TV studios, fussing over her, watching her retrace the exact same steps I had taken while campaigning for her.

But she handled herself beautifully. She looked well-presented, sporting a polka-dot top under a pink cardigan: the perfect image of a middle-class British woman. 'I blame myself for Richard's death. I will always blame myself for that, but I also blame myself for getting so involved with somebody who was able to control me,' she reasoned.

We had never really had this conversation, Mum and I. As I leaned into the small TV in the green room alone, I captured every word. It felt strange to learn her deepest thoughts here, of all places. 'Sally, if a woman is now watching this and hears the way you were controlled and it strikes a chord with what they're going through,' the presenter asked, 'what would you say to the women going through what you went through right now?'

'Tell somebody. Speak to somebody. Speak to a friend that you can trust, or a family member that you can trust, and they will help you to leave . . . You need to get out before it gets worse, because it will destroy you and destroy your children who have to watch that type of behaviour as they're growing up.'

A jolt of pride ran through me.

Into this mix of emotions came the strain of the Covid lockdowns, and not surprisingly James and Jen thought it might be better if Mum moved out. I was unhappy about

Mum being on her own in the middle of a global pandemic, but I couldn't really argue. They had all lived together for a whole year and the strain had become immense. James and Jen needed space alone to become a family with their newborn son.

For a time, Mum rented a house, but it felt bare and soulless to her, and didn't have much of a garden. It was a reminder of Ashton Place, where she had felt so bereft and rudderless.

I wanted it to be like the real old times, so I would offer to cook Sunday lunch. It was fun laughing and cooking together, fussing about the oven temperatures. It was a glimpse of her old self. She eventually bought a house not far from James and Jen. I went to stay with her for a few days shortly after she moved in – John and I were having some difficulties and I wanted to give us both space. On the first night, she went to bed quite early. As I drifted off to sleep, I could hear her on the phone talking late into the night. She mentioned that she had been chatting to Del. He had always been supportive: he had visited her when she had been in prison and also wrote to her, even appearing in the documentary. She had told me he was coming over to visit from LA.

Next morning at breakfast, the main topic of conversation was Del's impending visit. Mum was in a pensive mood. It was as though she was circling round something. Finally, she took the plunge: 'David, how would you feel if Del and I were a bit more than friends?'

Since last night I had subconsciously been waiting for this moment. I didn't quite know what to say. Soon after, I went home to John.

At the weekend, two days after Del had arrived, Mum and I planned to go and visit Michel, my uncle Brian's partner, together. Brian had recently died of Covid.

'We're setting off now,' she said. 'We'll be with you in about an hour. We can all go to Michel's together from your flat.'

We?

As soon as I heard that syllable, I realised she meant that Del was coming, and it blindsided me. Somehow I hadn't expected him to be present immediately at a private family moment.

It tipped me over into paralysis. Mum and Del were, right at this moment, in a car travelling towards my home. It catapulted me into a maelstrom of feelings not just about Mum, but about Dad too. Another man suddenly standing in his shoes.

I became overcome with anxiety just at the thought of Del inside my flat – it was my place of refuge. I just hadn't prepared myself. It was less than two years since Mum had been released. It was too much.

When they came, I couldn't face it: 'I'm not ready,' I said on the phone as they stood below on the doorstep. 'I don't want to let you in. I don' t want to let him in. I can't.'

Eventually they left, and I let them go to Michel's without me.

I couldn't compose myself afterwards. The very next day, a message from Mum appeared on my phone: *David, I really need to speak to you.*

I tried to keep it to text, not trusting myself to have a calm conversation: *What is it?*

No, I need to speak to you on the phone.

Bracing myself, I called her. 'What's going on, Mum?'

'It's Del. He's proposed to me. And I said yes.'

What?

I tried to explain that our family was only just putting itself back together. That I had thought she realised the toll the last decade had taken on us, that all these were trials we had weathered together. That I thought we all understood each other's trauma.

How could she even think of marrying a man we barely knew?

'What are you talking about, David? You know him. It's Del.'

'Mum, I've met him twice in my entire life, and one of those times I was eleven. Of course I don't know him.'

The conversation set off earthquakes in my foundations.

Maybe you don't know how I feel after all. The overriding emotion I felt on hearing about Del's proposal was panic. That panic was heightened because I had got into real personal trouble of my own. The year before, I had come into some money because of a legal case concerning Dad's estate. This was money that should have set me up for life. Money that should have allowed me and John to buy a house. A home. Everything I had ever wanted for us.

Instead, I had made one of the worst mistakes of my life. When the lockdowns started, with my hands idle and my mind numb from what came before, I decided to start trading the money on the financial markets. I had been drifting since Mum had been released. Struggling to accept there was still something broken within us. At first, trading felt like holding power and purpose over my problems. I remembered the evenings Dad had sat at his computer, investing in shares. Now, I felt like I was holding the wheel at last, shaping a future he couldn't touch. Part of me wanted to prove myself to my father. I wanted to make something for myself. I remembered how he used to cackle at me: 'You'll get nothing when I die, I'll have spent it all.'

Now I could make my fortune too. I could sanitise his inheritance, somehow. I thought that the more I won, the more I could stand against the memory of my father. And at first, I did. I remember there was a moment early on, when I was up an enormous amount, that I felt one of the biggest highs I had ever felt: absolutely on top of the world. On top of my problems. Finally, my life seemed to be my own.

And then I became brash and reckless, risked everything I had. I took out loans, threw in my life savings.

For weeks, I couldn't sleep. Every night I found myself lying awake, paralysed with fear. My mind frenetically spun with worry, turning over and over. I knew what I was doing. I knew what I was risking. But I had convinced myself I could still turn it around, that something would change, that I could make it all back. It was an obsession, a compulsion I had lived with unrelentingly for seven months. Everything in my world had become a sideshow. My work, my life with John. I had swapped out one trauma for another. And then, one night, the inevitable. It all collapsed, folding in on itself.

John had noticed. He always noticed. That morning, he reached out.

'Is everything okay, I know you didn't sleep well?'

'I don't want to talk about it,' I said.

I told him I'd just had a bad night, that I was stressed. But in reality, I had sat in the dark, my phone in my hands, watching as it all happened in real time. My positions crashing, the markets all moving against me. In the space of a few hours, it was all gone. I was frozen. My body went cold. I couldn't breathe. I wanted to undo it, to wake up and for it to be a nightmare. But there was nothing I could do.

Instead, I got up, walked in a daze to the study, sat there for a while, staring at nothing. Then I climbed back into bed next to John and lay still, eyes open, waiting for the morning. Hoping it wouldn't come.

And when it came, I couldn't move. I couldn't face it. It was early December, winter was already upon us, the outside grew colder with each day, and Christmas beckoned. John told me to meet him on his lunch break for a coffee, to get up and come to him.

'I'm a mess,' I said.

'We'll fix it,' he replied. 'Just get up and get dressed.'

So I did.

We met in the park in Chiswick, on a cold wooden bench. I didn't know how to start. I couldn't believe that at the end of all this I was sitting here. His face knew before I told him.

'It's all gone.'

'All of it?' he asked.

I folded my lips as though I could keep the words in. Then I let them out. 'Pretty much, yes.'

I looked at his face, wondering if it had landed. But he was just staring out into the distance. His eyes were unable to meet mine.

'I was leveraging,' I said, finally coming clean. 'I put everything into it. I borrowed vast sums. I'm sorry I didn't tell you. I'm so sorry.'

It was all I could keep saying. I had to stop myself. It felt like I was just vomiting one word after the other.

We sat for what felt like an eternity. People walked past us with their dogs. Walking. Their worlds still moving. Ours marooned in this moment, caught in the undertow of what I had done.

He exhaled sharply but didn't speak. He just sat back, processing, staring into the distance.

The silence was deafening. When I closed my eyes, flashes of Dad leaped out at me.

What would he make of this?

I wanted John to shout, to ask me how I had let it get this far. But instead he just said, 'Okay. We'll fix it.' Maybe that was his way of coping – I didn't know. I didn't want to pull at that thread, I just wanted to believe him.

There was no anger, no accusations, just quiet resolve. That was what made it worse. I knew what I deserved. I had placed another spectre, another dark cloud, on someone I loved the most.

Mum's big announcement, coming on top of all of this, made me feel like reality was shearing away from under me. I was spiralling. All the memories were suddenly raw again. I needed breathing space, and was lucky that I was going away for a few days with Ian. I limited my contact to a couple of texts to the family, making an agreement for us all – Mum, Del, me, James and Jen – to meet up and thrash everything out in a few days after I returned.

I was on a train just outside the city when a call came through from Jen. 'Did you know about this?' she said.

'Know what?' I asked.

'The wedding. They're planning to get married immediately. They've booked it for two days after you get back.'

'What?'

'Yes, it's all in place, apparently.'

'How could they do that? What about our family meeting? That's the day before. What the hell is the point of meeting if they're just going to go ahead the next day?'

The whole fragile edifice of my calm shattered. I knew why Mum was behaving erratically – she had a history of doing so. But was it not possible for her to just wait a little bit, for us to catch up and get used to the idea, now that things were finally finding some kind of fragile balance?

The following days unfolded in a maelstrom of calls and texts criss-crossing our entire family and circle, pulling in aunts and uncles, old counsellors and old friends. Even Harriet got involved. This was a woman barely two years free from prison, entering her first serious relationship as an adult with multiple mental disorders. I tried to get everyone to talk some sense into her and convince her to take some time to think such an important decision through. No one managed to dent her resolve. It was impossible for us all not to worry about her mental state.

But he makes me happy. Don't you want me to be happy?

This was her ace card. She'd had so much unhappiness, and now here it was, the fairytale ending. Her 'dash for happiness', she called it.

There was even a romantic backstory, one she told everyone: how Granny Jenney had apparently told Del years ago to 'look after Sally'. She pitched them as star-crossed lovers, finally able to be together in the twilight of their lives. They had both been through difficult times and now here they were, on the other side of it all, together. It was meant to be.

She planned to change her name too, saddling only us with the family name and the shame of it all.

'This is a private relationship, David,' she told me. 'You need to respect that.'

It was clear that any conversation we had with her from then on would be had with Del as well. Round and round we went, hour after hour. She simply couldn't understand why we were standing in her way.

'You know I love you, David. That's all that matters,' she would say, constantly.

'All we're asking is for six months to get to know him.'

I had never felt such emotional betrayal. I crumbled. Finally, I found myself giving her an ultimatum. Anything I could do to make her stop and think. 'Look, I cannot tell you how emotionally betrayed I feel. If you get married this quickly, I don't know if I can ever see you again. Are you prepared to take that risk?'

'I don't believe you'll do that, David. But if that happens, I am prepared.'

Something in me needed to hear her say those words. That was my out from a situation that had no exit.

Shortly afterwards I received a call from Harriet. 'I heard you said you'd never see her again. I think you're going too far, David.'

But I couldn't stop trying. I called her GP, asking if there was anything they could do, knowing her erratic behaviour was a symptom of her disorders. They made a referral to a Mental Health Crisis team that never happened. I even spoke to the vicar who was going to marry them. He told me he had promised to marry them and that, legally, he had to fulfil that promise. As I pulled every emergency lever I could, I finally resorted to lodging a police report. None of it came to anything.

The day of the wedding, John and I sat in our flat together. 'Has it happened? I guess it's happened,' one of us said. And that was it.

Chapter Twelve

Two years came and went. I spent them campaigning about coercive control through charity work and journalism. The memories of the children in the prison waiting rooms, running into the arms of their mothers, had stayed with me. I couldn't fix what had happened to Mum, but I could still try to help others.

I tried to reconnect with Mum a couple of times, in the hopes she would have now settled in to her whirlwind marriage. We spoke on the phone a little, and I even admitted something of the state I had got myself into. But I wanted to see her alone, and her flat response was always the same: 'I can't, I'm sorry.' Every time I read those words, it crushed me.

Finally, I gave in and agreed to visit her at Michel's with Del. I got as far as the front door. I raised my hand to ring the bell, but I just couldn't do it. I walked away.

Finally, one day she rang me up to say: 'How about you and I meet alone?'

We arranged to meet up in Kensington. I was early, and sat outside to wait. And then I saw her approaching, a tiny figure in a bright blue anorak. She had aged even more in the two years since I had last seen her.

She smiled as she approached, pulling me in to give me a big kiss on the cheek.

'Come here, my boy. It's so good to see you,' she said, sitting down.

I opened my pack of cigarettes. After all my hectoring, I had now taken up smoking myself – lighting up was a tiny act of self-destruction. 'Oh, David,' she said.

'I know, right? It's absurd. But hey, look at us now!' I replied, and we both tried to light our tobacco as the wind picked up.

We sat there, smoking together in the sunshine, with a heavy silence permeating the air.

It was hard to talk in the light of day. Even during the prison years, we had kept our darkness from one another in the hope of helping the other survive. That was our pact. We both tried to piece together words, like we were learning how to speak again.

'Del feels he hasn't done anything wrong,' she began. 'You don't have to accept him as your father or stepfather. He just wants to be accepted by you as my husband.'

I paused, taking it in. This felt like a high-stakes negotiation. I wanted to get it right because she had made her choice, and for the first time, it was truly her own, as a free woman. I wanted to be better, to hear her.

'I appreciate that,' I said, trying to find a centre ground. 'Look, none of us in our family have ever really sat around to speak about our emotions, through any of this.' I shifted in my chair, unable to make eye contact. 'You know why I refused to see you with Del?'

'Why?' she asked.

'Because . . . it was traumatising. Another man next to

you, so closely tied to Dad. For you, he represented salvation. For me, loss. I was losing you again, to another man.'

As I looked back at her now, her eyes locked onto mine. Her gaze was uncomfortable, but attentive.

'I understand your emotions, David. I understand,' she said. 'You know I love him though, don't you?'

'Yes, I understand,' I replied. 'I know.'

The words felt like a bridge. Fragile, but there.

It felt like we were starting to see each other at our cores. Accepting one another. She began to talk about life in prison.

'Things happened to me . . .'

I listened for over an hour as she shared more of her life behind those walls. How she had felt suicidal. How she had been bullied. Her hyper moments, her very down ones – how hard it had been to endure them all.

'Working in the gardens was my release,' she said, lost in the memory.

I imagined her finding peace tending to the flowerbeds in prison ground, just as she had at Ruxley Ridge.

Somehow it was comforting to talk about this, now that it was in the past. Restorative.

'You know why it was hard for *me* to share about my life without you?' I asked.

She nodded, 'I know. I asked about it because, well . . . I never wanted to speak about my life either.'

Her mouth inverted, the same crescent moon shape. We had let too much time slip.

Finally, I tried to find understanding. 'I know why you did it, why you rushed to marry him. I get it. You had your freedom back and . . . this was you exercising that. Exercising your freedom.'

After an hour of talking, she said what I had known she would. 'Why don't you come back to the flat? Del's there. He'd love to see you.'

I put my head in my hands for a moment before standing up. 'Fine, let's do it. Now or never.'

It felt like an armistice.

Del was standing in the entrance as we entered the flat. I walked straight up to him. 'Hi,' I said. 'How are you?' I hugged him. It wasn't easy. Everything in me tensed, but I pushed through it because I needed to. I had to let something go.

'Let's go for a Sunday roast tomorrow,' she said. 'All together.' It felt good to park everything, to put it aside. So we went for lunch, and it was good. A nice, normal gathering.

But my demons hadn't left me. I was still trading. And I had started borrowing to cover myself. I was clinging to the vain hope that I could get back what I had lost.

I was now checking my phone 50 to 100 times a day, watching my trading either pay off or dwindle my funds further. I was hiding what I was doing from everyone, blindly believing that just around the corner my luck would change. My emotions were tied to the ups and downs of my luck. It destroyed me – or rather, I destroyed myself. I drove myself into a wall and I couldn't for the life of me work out how and why I had got there.

Mum had tried to help me out. I didn't ask for money, and I didn't want it from her. But she had made a transfer into my account, and then I had done the most predictable thing in the world: I lost it again.

Neither of us knew how to name what was really happening to me, to stare my trading in the face and call it what it was: gambling. We were both ill-equipped to handle what was brazenly in front of us, too used to surviving our own crises, too practised at papering over the cracks.

I hate to think of the things I did at the time: the money I borrowed from my brother, and the time I pawned my uncle's gold watch that Michel had given me, the kind of heirloom that I should have guarded forever. Standing in a pawnshop handing it over, I felt a darkness press down from behind me onto my shoulders, a shame for where I was and how I'd got there. A new level of isolation, suffocating me like never before. I was out of control, alone with my addiction. When I confessed to John that I had relapsed, it was more than he could cope with and, not surprisingly, we split up. There had to be a line eventually. And that was it.

I sat alone in my flat that evening. I had lost everything I could afford to lose. And I had lost John, the one thing I couldn't afford to lose. The walls seemed to close in around me. A familiar darkness narrowed in.

My friend Carlos responded to a desperate text I sent him that night. He sent a cab to pick me up and told me to get in it. He and his wife Vicky took me in. Their three-year-old, Oliver, my godson, called my name as I came through the door. He ran to me and I dropped my bags and fell to the floor as he gave me a huge hug.

The next day I sought help from a gambling charity and they immediately put me on a programme of therapy that helped me walk back from the brink. In the end, I was saddled with debt. My own debt to repay. I had to fix it all – it had to be me that did it. It took time, but I eventually paid my brother back. I got the watch back from the pawnbroker – that cost me every last penny, but it was worth it. I managed my debts, and kept my head above water.

When I began to come up for air, I started to spend time in spaces of recovery, connecting with other addicts. I was struck by how many of them had witnessed domestic abuse in the home as a child; how men who gambled were statistically more likely to have suffered childhood traumas. The same kinds of traumas that had loomed over the landscape of my life.

I succumbed to a cold realisation: that I had spent my whole life running. From my past. From my present. From the spectre of my father. From the unspoken sadness and anger that still lingered around my mother. I had convinced myself that some dream future was better than my reality, so I lived in it. I allowed myself to believe in it, and allowed myself to be exploited by it. But the truth was, it was always just a dream. The music had ended, and there was nowhere left for me to go. I had to stop.

John and I finally met up again. As I looked at him, I could see how much of the weight of my trauma he had carried over the last years. I knew that asking him to shoulder my addiction had been a burden too far. But we sat in our living room, and I poured out what I had left in me.

'I love you enough to want you to be happy, I really do,' I said. 'If that's with me or without me. I did this, I've brought everything traumatic in your life to your door. And though

I know my trauma is not all my own fault, I'm responsible for my own actions. There must be an end to it, the end I've promised for so long. To be happy. I just want you to be happy, and if that's not with me, I accept that. I completely do.'

It was all I could offer him – and to my eternal gratitude, he accepted my apology and took me back.

Chapter Thirteen

'So, what would you like to talk about? Where would you like to go?' The therapist's voice was low, calm.

'Do I talk about how I lost it all, or how I'm coping in general? Sorry, this is all quite new to me,' I replied, faltering.

'Whatever you want, David. We can talk about anything.'

'I guess, I . . .' I took a moment to pause, overwhelmed at the scale of the question,

I was crawling back from the abyss I had been in. But as I sat in the therapist's chair, I was still lost in shame. I threw accusations at myself. A squanderer. A deadbeat. A failure.

'I had a future, and I gambled it away,' I said at last. 'And, well, I'm confused. I don't know why. Why did I do that? How did I get here?'

I had thought I understood my story, and the traumas that came with it. But I realised that I hadn't. I had failed to process any of it. Instead, I had buried it all like toxic waste beneath my feet. Now it was seeping out and into my life again. I knew I had to try and find him again: little David. Therapists over the years had repeatedly asked me to, but I couldn't. When Dad was buried, so too was my childhood. But now I was ready. In my heart, I knew there was only one place left to go. So I went back; back to the start. Back to the child I was.

I found that child in a memory, and all the anger and confusion finally left my body. I was far out, somewhere remote and strange-looking, where we used to go. A long-forgotten place at the edge of it all.

In my imagination it was a castle-grey day. The rough winds swirled in every direction, disrupting my senses, but I could just about make out the masses of green fringing the tops of the dunes.

Camber Sands.

In my mind the vast, five-mile expanse sprawled out in front of me, and there he was in the distance, clear as day, playing on the beach. Little David. Bleached blond hair with a cowlick and permanent grin across his face.

There was a time when I was a happy child, full of life, a million words spilling out at once, dreams of the things I'd grow to be. A child who would talk to anyone who would listen; who laughed easily and saw the world as a place to explore. But he was taken from me, submerged beneath the weight of things no child should have to endure or could ever describe.

I smiled to myself, realising I had finally unlocked this memory at the core of it all. In it, little David laughed, running towards my mother. I could see it clearly: the two of us together locked in time, the memory untouched, unspoiled by what came before and what lay after.

Just as though the sun had pierced through the clouds, scenes of early childhood happiness started cascading into my mind like a waterfall. Fun fairs, dungarees, birthday parties, squeals of childish joy, splashing in a pool. All wrapped up in a pure love. The love that I had as a child, which had got lost along the way.

It felt like I was bringing him home. Restoring something in me that had been taken. Repatriating a part of my soul.

The warmth of that love seemed to stay with me afterwards.

In the years that followed, my mother and I dismantled the final bricks in the wall that had long stood between us. We were coming back from the years at sea. We saw each other again for lunches and days out. She was no longer unreachable, and we found our way back into each other's lives. She my mother, and I her son.

She was now a phone call away at any time, in her new home with its beautiful garden, a sanctuary of plants and flowers. Families of wild peacocks visited her often. Some say they're a symbol of strength, power and freedom.

I was confronting the past, transcribing the harms that had been scrawled in my mind and writing it between the covers of a book as a means of survival. My health and happiness returned. My relationship with John became stronger.

But sometimes I could still feel the shadows of the past overtaking me.

'David, can I ask you . . . what does happiness look like for you?' my therapist asked me one day.

I thought of my home. My little flat, my refuge. But it had come from the money I had inherited from Dad. He was embedded in every room, in its very structure. Mum was embedded in the pots and pans lining the kitchen. Deep down, it all reminded me of my trauma.

But as I spoke, I realised another truth: my idea of happiness was born from a place that I had promised myself I would never go back to. A seemingly picture-perfect place where I had always struggled to feel that happiness, and never felt it bloom into life.

Epilogue

Alone and without plans one bright sunny weekend, I decided to take myself out of the noise of the city. The destination didn't matter; I just wanted to find some peace. I was standing in a familiar spot on the concourse of Waterloo station, staring blankly at the destination board, when the inevitable happened. The train service to Claygate blinked up in front of me. It still existed. *Of course it still existed.*

I tried to look at other destinations, but I could feel it up there on the board. Refusing to blink out of existence.

There was no thought in my mind beyond walking to the platform and boarding the train. The train slowly rolled out of the station as the tall shiny buildings of London slowly faded into nothingness. They waved me out to the suburbs, back to the leafy village I came from.

The itinerary felt like a tour of my adolescence, the stops still all the same. Earlsfield, where Mum took me for guitar lessons in my mid-teens. Surbiton, where Mum worked for the Police Federation. Then darker memories started to swirl. Lurking behind Surbiton station was the brothel where Mum had caught Dad. The building had since been demolished, but its spectre still loomed large. I imagined the women who had lived behind those doors, in the flats Dad frequented. Women trafficked and abused for men like my father to use.

The train sped on. And before I was ready, I found myself

standing on the platform at Hinchley Wood. Granny Jenney's home. I had not visited this place since she died. A place of happy memories, of sanctuary for Mum and for me.

First, I went into the sweet shop. The one where Mum would give me a pound coin and allow me to pick out the total value of sweets as a test of my maths skills. They still had the same dark brown, wood-grained bowls from my childhood, and even some of the same sweets. The jellied worms and the disco sherbets. The newspaper shop where Dad and Mum had met had been just here, in this parade of shops.

Granny's home didn't look much different either. The same front door, the front garden just a bit more overgrown. It felt like I could walk up and she might still come to the door.

Before long, I felt the main road calling me away to face the inevitable homecoming. I started my walk to Claygate, the sun high in the midday sky as if it knew why I was here.

The landscapes and roads all felt familiar. The bumps, ridges and flow of the pavement formed a familiar and comforting topography beneath my feet. The smell of freshly cut grass. The low whirring of lawnmowers in the distance. It all welcomed me back. I had forgotten how beautiful these homes were, how picturesque.

And then a deafening silence. My heart sank as I walked up the road: Ruxley Ridge.

I peered down to see my old home burrowed at the far end of the driveway. It was more concealed than before; preened hedges now restricted the view down.

It would still be a nice place to have a family.

In my childhood, domestic abuse existed only on my

television screen. Everything had told me it belonged somewhere else. Not somewhere like here, with its pristine frontages, its order and sense of calm. It existed with women who were visibly battered and bruised, a long way from my world. And yet it was here. Invisibly. The lull of peace and shrouded privacy here concealed the danger that lay within. It was not a place where control was seen as abuse. But that meant it was the perfect place for it to flourish, fester and grow wild. Coercive control is not about stopping you from speaking out, it's about ensuring you never think to speak in the first place.

Everything here appeared undisturbed, in order. But I knew more than anyone that any home could be a space of control. I remembered how cut off it felt down there. How lonely it was in that home.

I did love my dad, once. And there must be some love there still. I have the memories that belong to the little boy that I once was. But Dad made Mum into something she wasn't, twisted her mind out of all recognition. He broke her.

Yet despite all this, he didn't deserve to die.

An early memory pulls me back to somewhere in France, when I was very little. We were outside a café – me, Mum and Dad – when a horrible car crash happened on the other side of a bridge. Dad ran to help, and I screamed for him, again and again. My mother held me from running after him, and I kicked and kicked in her arms at the thought he would get hurt. I never wanted him to get hurt.

Now he lives somewhere in my face: I see glimpses of him when I look in the mirror. I used to feel sick at that thought. He was a man who did awful, terrible things, but he is my father. I don't know if there will ever be a final resting place in my memories.

Looking at the house on Ruxley Ridge, I tried to imagine a different story. One in which I could find a way to speak to my father. One where he stopped. One which accepted that what he did was wrong. One where he would serve a sentence for something that is – now – illegal.

That reality doesn't exist for me. But it can exist for someone else.

I never wanted my family's story to be the one society needed to understand the sprawling destruction that coercive control wreaks. And for years, I resisted any label of victim. Or even survivor. It felt wrong. What I had lived through felt too messy for neat, clipped words. Yet Dad's abuse was an assault on all of us. The damage he did is permanent.

When coercive control was finally given a name, it helped me fight for my mother. But once I had done that, I had to fight for myself too. And eventually for others.

So I allowed myself the words. To say that I, too, am a survivor. There is a kind of freedom in that.

I looked at Ruxley Ridge one last time, the picture-perfect doll's house façade. It stayed in my mind as I turned and walked away, back to the station and to my own life, turning my back to the wood, the garden, the drive, the tall hedges, the front door, the past.

Afterword

3,000 historic murder convictions are currently being reassessed by the Criminal Cases Review Commission following the landmark case of my mother, Sally Challen, focusing on instances where coercive control was not previously considered as a factor. At least five cases have already been reopened, offering a glimmer of hope to those still trapped by the failings of the justice system.

In July 2023, Sally's Law was introduced, a reform requiring courts to recognise coercive control as a mitigating factor in cases of domestic homicide.

800,000 children are known to be affected by domestic abuse. But how many are still unaccounted for and left unseen? How many would grow up with traumas, the harm engraved into their bodies and their minds? How many would internalise that abuse and normalise it? How many would follow a path to addictions or self-harm? The scale of damage seems unfathomable, unthinkable.

Acknowledgements

To the women who lifted my voice from the shadows and who held me up when I didn't know how to stand, who understood my trauma before I had the words to name it. Your solidarity, wisdom and learning helped carry me forwards.

To the women like my mother, still waiting to be heard. And to the connected families carrying the weight of their silence.

To the adult child survivors who reached out to me, who let me know that witnessing abuse is to endure it, and that we, the children of these homes, are not just bystanders, but co-victims of these crimes. You helped me feel found and gave me belonging.

To Justice for Women, who to this day stand beside women and families left voiceless and powerless, fighting for justice where the system fails. And to the great Harriet Wistrich, whose unrelenting, stoical belief never wavered. To Clare Wade KC for her determination and strength. To Julie Bindel, whose enduring commitment to justice has lit the way for so many.

To Dalla, who first reached out to Harriet Wistrich in 2011, setting everything in motion, and to her husband Hugo, whose support carried me through.

To the women's charities who rallied around me. To those journalists who saw beyond the headlines, listened with care and believed in responsible reporting. To the politicians who stood by my family.

To the late Dr Evan Stark who gave me language to understand what had once felt like words in the dark. His legacy endures in every life his insights have touched. And to the many trauma-informed experts whose work continues to deepen our understanding of domestic abuse and who work to stop the escalation of harm.

Special thanks to Jo Unwin, who, when I sat in front of her all those years ago, saw me for the survivor I was long before I could see it myself. Who gave me the courage to believe that my voice and my story mattered. And who stuck by me to the end. To Celia, for her quiet guidance that brought clarity when, at times, the past felt too heavy to hold. To Teresa Parker, who showed me that my mother's story was not just my mother's, nor mine alone, it belonged to so many other women, and I was not alone.

To the people in addiction recovery groups, who welcomed me into their spaces and trusted me with their own stories. Who showed me that harm doesn't exist in a vacuum, that it takes root in childhood and spreads in ways we often can't control and we still strive to recognise. You helped me understand myself in ways I never had before. To Nick, who brought me back from the brink of those battles and helped me believe that happiness exists for me.

To the friends who never knew how to handle my trauma, but were always patient. To every member of the public who shared their own personal stories with me. Your belief in me, in this fight, has meant more than I can put into words.

And to the children who today grow up in the silence, for those who are wrongly taught that coercion and control are acts of love, for those who might one day piece together their own stories from the harm they never asked for.

To my brother, who trusted and stood by me in our campaign together.

To John, who always saw that happy boy in me and never let him go. Who weathered every storm by my side.

And finally, to my mother. This book would not exist without your faith in me, without the journey we have travelled together. It is a testament to the life we have fought for, the truth we have reclaimed, and the love that has endured it all.

This brazen book was created by

Publisher: Romilly Morgan
Acting Publisher: Ella Gordon
Development Editor: Celia Hayley
Senior Developmental Editor: Pauline Bache
Editorial Assistant: Emily Campbell
Creative Director: Mel Four
Copyeditor: Laura Gladwin
Senior Production Manager: Katherine Hockley
Sales: Isobel Smith
Publicity & Marketing: Ailie Springall and Charlotte Sanders
Legal: Rhiannon James